HATING THE CINNAMON ROLL CEO

A CINNAMON ROLLS AND PUMPKIN SPICE ROM-COM

by

CAMILLA EVERGREEN

To my dearest, sweetest Stormie.
Who would never sacrifice anyone at all, ever.
~*~

Reader Expectations

Heat Level: Fade-to-black, innuendos, no cursing, sensual description, mentions of sex

Notable Tropes: Enemies to lovers, office romance, reverse grumpy/sunshine, only one bed, opposites attract, billionaire, cozy gamer girl?

Triggers: dementia, grief, mentions of suicide, death threat jokes - which is perfectly normal healthy relationship behavior I'm sure

Style: First person present, dual POV

Stress Level: Low

Ending: HEA

Prologue

Avoid mixing alcohol with the internet.

– Marcella

Question 1: Full Legal Name

Taking another sip from my bottle of wine, I squint drearily at my laptop screen. My cursor blinks in the text box below question numero uno. Full…legal…name…

I swear into the glass when the answer hits me. "I totally know that one."

After misspelling my name twice, I manage to input *Marcella Reina Keyes.*

It takes me another full minute to recall my birthday, but only because I'm a little too inebriated to remember it's *today.*

August 8th.

Prime smack in the armpit of a Georgia summer.

Behind me in the cramped living room of my overpriced garbage apartment, my feeble window AC unit coughs and chokes, none the wiser that my will to live rests solely upon its frail mechanical shoulders. There's a fight taking place somewhere downstairs. Upstairs, my neighbor's three children protest their bedtime. Loudly. With significant jumping.

If I weren't so focused on filling out this form, I'd send

a drunk text to my mother, apologizing for my existence. Bless that woman if I ever had the lung capacity to reach the octaves my neighbor's kids are managing.

The cacophony reaches right through my noise-canceling headphones, which are blaring music directly into my ear cavities.

Maintaining such piercing sounds is an achievement, truly.

Question 6: Describe your perfect date.

The urge to put *April 25* in reference to *Miss Congeniality* comes nearly as violently as the urge to put *not August 8*.

Thankfully, I come to my senses and recall that this question isn't referring to a calendar date. It's referring to a date *date*. Like, going to the movies. Or long walks on the beach.

Which.

For the record.

Took me twenty-six years to realize meant *getting to know a person one-on-one*. Not just having the inexplicable urge to get sand in your shoes and salt in your hair for a prolonged length of time. Apparently.

In case anyone's wondering, I've had this knowledge for a marvelous four minutes.

Because, yes, I'm googling date ideas and wishing I could blame the absence of a clue on my half-full bottle of wine. In all reality, I don't do much. I have never *done much*. I go to work. I come home. I play *Stardew Valley* with my best friends.

That's it.

I'm not even out doing anything today because my goal in life is blissful anonymity, and birthdays are an antagonist of that noble effort. Being the center of attention just because I was born once upon a time is ridiculous. Even my darling friends know better than to so much as text me today.

Dates… Dates… Dates…

The few dates I've been on were wholly uneventful. Classic. Boring. Predictable.

Movies and coffee shops and just *hanging out*, with Netflix on.

Which is another thing that took me an embarrassing amount of time to understand.

Thankfully, the definition hit me like a bullet train when that guy from my high school's hand found my waist. I got out of that scummy boy's parent-free environment before his disgusting mouth reached mine. If I'm not mistaken, I threw the remote at him, too. He seriously didn't even let me finish picking a movie.

What a louse.

Sighing, I remember I bought myself a cake at Publix— along with this bottle of wine. Even though I don't formally celebrate my birthday, the single constant is that I use the excuse to get myself a little guilt-free treat. This year, my *guilt-free treat* is an entire lemon curd and vanilla cake with buttercream frosting.

The beautiful little personal cake peers at me from the kitchenette counter beyond the armrest of my couch, where my feet are propped so my newly-painted toenails can finish drying. They are alternating red and black, ending on ladybug big toes. I wiggle them, sigh, and figure I should finish this form question before I reward myself with the cake.

Perfect date.

Perfection is an unattainable standard, given that human imperfection causes the definition to perpetually shift from one moment to the next. There are several specific things I enjoy doing, but there are many people I

3

would not enjoy doing them with. I suppose the same can be said in the opposite direction. A perfect date is the person, not the activity. If the activity must determine whether or not I enjoy myself, I'm probably with the wrong person, but if the activity would make me want to scream without the support of my company, they might just be perfect.

I double-check with good ol' Google to make sure this question does indeed refer to the activity, not the description of the person with whom dates are partaken, then I move on.

Somewhere after question twenty, I run out of wine and remember my cake, so I drag myself off the couch and snatch it. Fork primed with an entire buttercream frosting rose, I march on.

Question 34: How do you handle disagreements?

Full sugary goodness fills my mouth while I do a spot of soul searching.

When was the last time I found myself plagued by a disagreement I had to *handle*?

I have two friends.

Two.

And I've kept them around all these years because they don't prompt unnecessary things like *disagreements*. There's a right way and a wrong way to everything. Whenever we hit something that looks suspiciously like the start of a disagreement, we talk like adults until we learn what's correct.

At...work...this method of *communication* is not accessible.

Because work is full of pretentious idiots.

But that's another thing entirely.

I relay my preference for talking things out when possible, and my tendency to bottle up my frustrations when otherwise. Specifically at work. Due to all the idiots.

Disagreements, I conclude in the form, *can only be resolved when all active parties are made of flesh and bone —not brick and plaster.*

"This is a dang good cake," I mumble.

Half of it has mysteriously disappeared.

So weird.

Almost as weird as these never-ending questions. Mercy.

Question 56: How much alone time do you need?

All of it. Every last drop. I juice that sucker like it's liquid gold. Since my job is frequently unpredictable and full of surprise travel, on the blessed days when I'm in the office during the usual nine-to-five, I require the remaining eight waking hours to myself. The harrowing reality that another day comes every morning makes my recharge time painfully important. Dare I say, necessary. For survival.

I enjoy a modest singular outing with my friends every two weeks to a month. And quite often, I neglect the group chat organizing such an outing until an embarrassing amount of time has passed. The thing is, I do enjoy going out with my friends. But I never go anywhere by choice on the days that I work. And I do tend to begin dissociating at around the eight hours of socialization mark.

Huh.

I guess that means, regardless of surrounding activities, I need a perfectly reasonable eight hours a day of alone time, not counting sleep.

Smirking, I type in my answer.

To think Mom and Dad called me antisocial throughout my childhood as though being *antisocial* isn't a full-time job.

Question 79: Where do you want to live?

Not here.

Somewhere with an excellent cooling and heating system. I'm talking somewhere I can afford sixty-nine degree temps indoors in the summer. Somewhere quiet. Somewhere with less light pollution than the dead center of Atlanta, which isn't a high bar given your social status, I know, but still. I think I'd like to see the stars every once in a while.

Question 93: Do you consider yourself to be high maintenance?

Absolutely not. Lock me in a room with snacks and the internet for a month. I will thrive.

Question 102: List all five love languages in order of which you find to be most to least important. You may explain if you so desire.

Love speaks more than five languages. It sees. It listens. It adapts. Sometimes, people need kind words. Sometimes, they need a coffee. Sometimes, they need to be held. I can't rate the importance of how love is expressed any more than I can rate water, food, and air. It's all important, in different quantities at different frequencies. It just depends on what you need in a given moment and, perhaps, how long it takes between getting what you need before you start to die.

Question 125: How do you deal with change or the unexpected?

Gracious. How many questions are there…?

I could scroll ahead.

But that would give me something to look forward to.

And we won't be having that.

I deal poorly with the unexpected. My response tends to include internal screaming, and I have been known to throw up. Just not recently.

Question 143: What constitutes cheating?

Acting dishonestly, unfairly, or unfaithfully.

It's the Google definition. Because I've never thought about defining cheating before. I don't understand why people cheat on the people they claim to love the most. I'd hate myself forever for betraying someone I care about or who cares about me.

Being cared about is a gift.

I'm not one to scorn a gift.

Question 199: Is there anything you'd like to add, say, or share before proceeding to the final question then consenting to submit these answers for the purposes defined previously? My assistant will be in touch with any answers to relevant queries should you be shortlisted.

That poor assistant. Having to deal with all the nonsense of this form, and now my own personal brand of nonsense. They deserve a raise.

I appreciate the thoroughness of this interrogation and the obvious desire to end on a solid 200. Out of curiosity, which questions were stuffed in just to meet that quota? Also, if shortlisted, do I receive a copy of your answers to all these questions? It only seems fair. If you couldn't tell, I'm not the biggest fan of power imbalances, and the scale already tips oh so heavily in your favor.

Question 200: Why do you want to marry me?

Finally. It's over. The sense of dull pride rising in my chest is wholly uncalled for, but here it is, bubbling up like fulfillment... Or, actually, that might be the entire cake I just ate. Who can say for sure?

Back to this delightful little question...

Why do I, a perfectly normal young adult, want to become the housewife of a random billionaire whose name I don't even know because I didn't bother checking anything before clicking your ad?

Simple.

Easy.
Painless, even.
I really, really hate my job.

Chapter 1

Drown me in a moat, please. I'd like to see a castle before I die.

– Marcella

Finnegan Marsh—AKA the bane of my existence, my boss, and a man whose only true merit is…just about everything about him—beams at me when I enter his office for our usual morning meeting. The only issue is: he prefaced today's meeting with a text that said he had something important he wanted to discuss. I'm growing all too familiar with how he operates, so I can confirm this morning's text is bad news. It's the *Never mind! Everything you've expected today is in the toilet. Flush. Now, we're going to Europe!* text, which could so easily be translated into a *Better to drive off a bridge than come into work* text.

It's a shame I've never been one to trust translations.

Blue eyes sparkling like fancy smancy champagne flutes, Mr. Marsh stands and presents the creaking leather chair in front of his obnoxiously large desk. The action strikes me as odd. Normally I just linger near enough to the door to judge the fact he has a koi pond in his floor and far enough from the door to bolt out of the way without winding up *in* the koi pond when he charges on by so we can pack.

I do not want to sit in the plasticky loud chair, but I do. I also do not want to smile, but I didn't spend many hours in my formative years practicing how to exude perfect calm and peace in the mirror for nothing, so tralala. I *love* being up at five every day in order to be at this frivolous man's beck and call.

It's my *favorite.*

Sure, being at his beck and call is—quite literally—the job I signed up for, and Marsh Industries pays me eighty grand a year to do it, but it's a human right to complain about one's employment, and I do enjoy pretending to be human.

Smile flawless, I say, "You wanted to speak with me about something important that has the potential to derail today's plans, Mr. Marsh?"

"How many times have I told you it's okay to call me *Finn*, Marcella?"

I hum and tilt my soulmate—the LeoPad tablet from Leopard Co. that I use to track literally everything *Mr. Marsh* does—away from my body. "Not sure, sir." My voice is light, airy, *sweet and musical.* I take immense inspiration from my beautiful friend Penny, who was a siren in another life. "Happy to find out for you, though. Would you like me to start keeping a tally now then draw up an estimate in a month that takes the past two months into consideration based on the statistics I learn?"

The corner of his mouth tugs into an effortlessly handsome smile as he scoots into his desk, plants his chin in his palm, and…scans me.

Mr. Marsh is a lot of things. Flippant. Boisterous. Impulsive. *Much* too…*smiley. Way* too *nice.* But he's absolutely not a creep. Or, at least, he hasn't been a creep for the past two months.

Perhaps I haven't been working here long enough to tell

for sure.

Prior to this position, I have several years of assistant experience that inform me the cliché about secretaries and their bosses…is rooted in the truth.

My perfectly practiced smile falters. "Mr. Marsh, why are you looking at me like that?"

Eyes widening, Mr. Marsh laughs, runs his fingers through the gleaming auburn strands of his hair, and says, "Sorry. You're beautiful, Marcella. I don't think I've ever noticed before."

I blink.

His words repeat in my skull.

My trained smile vanishes, one tiny tilt at a time.

Suddenly, I'm wearing my normal face in front of my boss, which is something I only do when I'm positive nobody important is watching. And when you're the personal assistant to the billionaire CEO of Marsh Industries, somebody important is *always* watching.

Swears hiss into my head, and I remind myself that overreacting is for wusses who don't like to pay their overwhelming debts. Channeling *unease* that bridges on *disgust*, I shift in the uncomfortable, crisp leather seat. "I'm very uninterested in anything my physical appeal might assist you with, Mr. Marsh. If this sort of topic comes up again, I will have to resign."

Without severance. As in, I will be suing for several million.

And probably losing since I can't afford a several-million dollar lawyer…

But, you know, delusion is a grand pastime of mine.

Mr. Marsh's brows rise.

I regain my peachy smile. "I don't mean to be harsh. I'm only here to do my job. I'm sure you understand. I didn't sign up for…anything else."

"I don't mean..." He cups a hand to his mouth, laughs into it. "Well, let me see if I can explain in a better way..." Before I get the chance to panic, he turns his attention toward his computer. "Ah. Here we go." The fine lines around his eyes crinkle when his smile returns in full.

Whenever I see wrinkles on his face, I remember he's thirty-two, not seven.

Even though he has the attention span of a rodent and I'm little more than his glorified nanny, he is a full-grown adult.

Even though I usher questions his way to keep him on task, put away all the emails he leaves out, make sure he eats, do all his planning, and *dress* him, sitting right in front of me is an entire adult man.

Coordinating someone's outfits to match the weather is not exactly what I thought would wind up on my schedule after I graduated from four years of business school.

Alas.

"Marcella Reina Keyes," he murmurs, swiping his thumb across his bottom lip as he peruses the text on his screen. The idea of a laugh puffs from his nose as he cuts a glance my way. "I did a thing."

My eyes close, briefly, and I do my very best not to sob.

Anytime Mr. Marsh *does a thing*, I need to readjust his plans, make new orders, cancel and confirm reservations, update his wardrobe for whatever climate he's decided we're ending up in. The entire ordeal involves usually twenty emails and thirty phone calls, all of which often occur on a private jet. Because, *what do you know*, he's planned a business deal in *Nepal*.

I've been here for two months.

I have seen more of the world than I have *ever* wanted to.

Whatever the opposite of wanderlust is—that's what I

12

have.

Stay home lust. *Leave me alone* lust. *For why* lust.

If not for that glorious, glorious salary, I would not still be here.

The only reason I chose *assistant* as my career path at all is because it's a position of *planning* and *telling people what to do*. I excel at both those things. It's just that... well...my excellence may vary where the most frustrating man in the world is concerned.

"Are you all right, Marcella?" he asks.

I swallow, hard, and open my eyes. Voice still pitched in my *customer service* tone, I say, "Of course. What have you done?" *This time*. What have you done *this time* that requires me to rip up everything in your calendar, you soulless ginger?

His fingers lock in front of his pouting lips, and there's almost a kind emotion in his eyes before they go chihuahua empty-bright once more. "I made an *advertisement*," he says, as though he has learned a new word.

I'd be proud of him.

If I cared.

"Incredible, sir." I look at my tablet again. "Should I get marketing involved? Send data somewhere for analyzation? Take—"

"For a wife."

My mind goes blank.

Achingly slow, I lift my attention off the tablet before me, meet Mr. Marsh's strikingly amused gaze, and barely whisper, "What?"

"I made an advertisement for a wife. *Wanted: Billionaire Housewife before Christmas.* Ring any bells?"

No. Not exactly. If I had to identify the sound going off in my head right about now, it's more like a siren. My mouth has gone utterly dry. Two weeks ago, on my

13

birthday, I got a little drunk and a little click happy with a stupid ad.

A very, very stupid, blindingly bright ad…

"Why…" I attempt to moisten my lips. "…didn't you tell me about this?"

"You had the day off. I got bored, and I was unsupervised…" He toys with a pen, and if he picks it up and starts *clicking it*, I will kill myself.

I wish I could say I'm surprised he *got bored* and started *advertising for a wife*. I'm just not. This man's *boredom* is the consistent fuel behind this entire industry's success. There's always a new deal to make, a new avenue to try, a new company to grow into the multi-millions.

I don't have to like the chaos to know it works.

After all, his chaos this time roped me in, didn't it?

Maybe I'm overreacting.

After all, where would *the* Finnegan Marsh get the time to sort through the hundreds of applications he no doubt got? This world is full of desperate idiots.

I just usually enjoy pretending I'm not one of them.

Being worried he knows I'm in the mess of applications shouldn't cloud my logic. I have to be overreacting.

I mean.

Okay.

Sure, he called me by my full name a few moments ago, but it has been *two weeks* since I filled out his form. Two weeks of applications is too many for a busy billionaire to handle. Not only that, the application ended on a question that said his *assistant* would be in touch.

I felt bad for that assistant.

Oh, the irony.

The full name thing was a coincidence. He just wants me to compile the shortlist.

Yup.

We will be adamantly ignoring the fact he opened this conversation with a compliment about my appearance.

Denial, another fond pastime. Snuggles right up next to delusion. I am a fan of the alliteration.

"So," I begin, the pinnacle of calm, "you'd like me to review applications? Is there any deeper purpose to this endeavor? Any deadline I should take into consideration? Will you lose a trust fund if you aren't married by a certain date?"

He stops messing with his pen and chuckles. "This isn't a romcom, Marcella."

"Oh. I'm sorry. I didn't mean to imply—"

"I'm just lonely."

Yet again, my poor brain skids to a halt and takes a moment to reboot. He's...lonely?

Him.

Seriously?

Him?

He's surrounded by people constantly, dragging me halfway across the world for dinners and overnight events and parties. He knows *people*. Point blank. He knows people from here, there, and everywhere. Worse, people know *him*. He's old money. Sole heir to a rich family heritage. He can't go anywhere without a couple bodyguards tailing him.

If he wants a wife because he's *lonely*, he has so many options it is laughable.

Why make a rush-deal form and advertise it at all?

"You seem shocked," he murmurs. "I'm not allowed to be lonely?"

Looking like a statue of Apollo? Um. No, I don't think so.

He's the complete package. For most people.

I prefer far more stability from the personalities I allow

around me.

Nevertheless, I say, "Of course you're allowed to be lonely, Mr. Marsh. Do you have any criteria for me to cross-reference as I go through applications?"

"No." Pushing back in his chair, he opens a drawer in his desk and pulls out a stack of papers regardless. "I suppose I haven't been perfectly clear. I've already gone through the applications."

My entire life flashes before my eyes. My heart jumps up my esophagus to lodge in my throat. Oh well. A living wage was nice, while it lasted. Seeing the end of my crippling debt on the horizon...give or take twenty years with a working AC unit, or nineteen without one...

What grand dreams.

"Marcella?"

Frail, I say, "Yes, sir?"

"Were you held at gunpoint when you waded through all two hundred questions? Right now, you seem somewhat...apprehensive."

My eyes close. "Do I?"

"Yes."

Goodness gravy. I do wonder if it has anything to do with all the crap I said about you in those two hundred answers. My apprehension is a real, real, sincere, complete mystery.

I force down a swallow. "My apologies. No, sir. I wasn't held at gunpoint."

"So you answered the form of your own free will?"

"I was drunk." Something inside me is dying. If I survive the rest of this conversation, it's going to take months for the scent to leave the crevices of my soul.

Mr. Marsh clicks his tongue. "I see. So it's safe to say you were more yourself than usual?"

I resent him.

16

So much.

Circling a fingertip atop the stack of papers he removed from the drawer, Mr. Marsh rests his mouth against his fist and peers at the computer screen. "I know I ran the ad on an account disconnected from Marsh Industries and maintained a level of anonymity, but I still thought perhaps you knew when I saw your name. Then I started reading your responses, and I thought perhaps you'd found a sense of humor when so many replies ridiculed your boss and bemoaned your position. But while they weren't all insulting, they were all detailed…" He moves his hand to his mouse and scrolls. "Insightful and earnest…" His expression softens, tender. "It was hard to believe it was a joke after a while. I suppose all I can say now is you hide how much you hate me very well."

I droop against the terrible fabric of this stupid, stupid, *stupid* chair. There's no point in trying to escape now. He has so much incriminating evidence sitting right in front of him. I am doomed. "It…takes a lot of effort."

"I imagine it does. Are you aware that for the question asking what traits you value in a man, you preface a list delineating my exact opposites with *anyone but Finnegan Marsh is honestly great?*"

My fingers close into the fabric of my pantsuit as I force myself not to fidget with the hem of my jacket. "Truthfully, the whole experience is somewhat blurry. I ate an entire cake on top of the wine."

Blissful, he laughs, watching me like I am the strangest creature in the world. "At one point, as an addendum, you put *I don't even know why I'm doing this. I'm pretty sure I hate billionaires.*"

I whimper. "If I'm fired, I can leave gracefully, Mr. Marsh. I'll sign for severance, so you know I won't sue."

Cheerful, he fixes me with the most baffled expression

in the world. Then he has the audacity to ask, "Are you mad? You're the best assistant I've ever had, ever *met*. I'd be a fool to let you go. Also, given the libel you submitted to an unknown source, I'd have more grounds to sue than you would. Regardless, really, suing me is unwise. What would you even sue me for? *Being too nice?*"

As a matter of fact, yes. Exactly that.

His positive attitude causes me consistent, undue emotional distress.

Chuckling, he regards me warmly. "Fire you." His head shakes, auburn waves falling across his forehead before he pushes them back. "Silly girl. If I do that, who will hire our wedding planner?"

I shut down. I come back online. "Pardon?"

"You are exactly the kind of girl I want to marry. Every last one of your answers is riveting, capturing me completely. I'll not get ahead of myself and suggest I've fallen in love with you, but I am desperate to get to know you better outside our professional setting as we make preparations for a ceremony at the end of November."

Balking, I stammer, "I... I'm terribly sorry. I mean no disrespect. It's just that you seem to be forgetting...I hate you?"

Smiling—like an idiot, might I add—he watches me, as though waiting for me to say something that matters.

I cover my mouth.

His smile tames, some, just enough to be disconcerting. "Am I misunderstanding? Did you or did you not apply to become an unknown billionaire's wife? And am I or am I not a billionaire?"

What's the corporate polite way to say, *you are a lunatic*? "Husbands and wives...they...you know."

He blinks. "Yes. Do you find my appearance as repulsive as my character? Personally, I consider you quite lovely in both respects."

My stomach does a wee twist. "I am having a rather visceral reaction to what you just said."

Without missing a beat, he pulls the small trashcan out from under his desk and passes it to me. "You did note that unexpected change could make you throw up. To be honest, I don't consider love and romance as important as companionship, so don't worry if you aren't attracted to me. I won't force you to do anything against your will."

Aren't attracted—

I'd have to be an amoeba not to recognize his physical appeal.

Like him, however, I also consider the emotional side to be of far more importance than anything *physical*. So. *Yeah.* That I hate his character is a gargantuan issue, I think.

My skin goes cold and clammy. My LeoPad slips out of my grasp, so I can cradle the offered trashcan in my arms. Is this biting sensation running down the back of my throat embarrassment? Dread? *Vomit?*

"You would have preferred marrying someone you didn't know?" he asks.

"I was *drunk*, Mr. Marsh. My options were *mess around online* or *cry into my birthday cake*. It was by no means a serious application. I think it would be for both our benefits if you neglected it entirely."

Mr. Marsh clears his throat. "I'm sorry. I'm just trying to understand. You wrote a collective ten thousand words into an application you weren't serious about?"

I scowl at him over my trashcan. "Everyone needs a hobby."

A short laugh escapes him. "You are enchanting."

"Agree to disagree."

"Please consider becoming my wife, Marcella. It's not a bad deal, and I can't help but keep coming back to the fact

19

all your annoyances with me aren't grounded in any negative behaviors."

Um. Yeah. Because Mr. Marsh is a little sparkling sunshine fairy in a bottle. But I am a storm cloud. "I respectfully decline."

"You mentioned having an awful lot of debt in one of the money questions I included."

I wince. "That sounds like the start of blackmail. Should I be recording this?"

He shrugs his broad shoulders, leans back, and twists side to side in his chair. "You may, if you'd like. However, legally, against me, you don't have a prayer."

He has a point. And it's sharp.

"I promise I'm not trying to blackmail you. It's just… Is being in my presence really as terrible as you've made it out to be?" he murmurs. "Just because I smile too often and am too energetic?"

My eyes narrow.

"You can tell me the truth. Your honest feelings don't bother me, and I think we're well past your good assistant act. I've never seen you be particularly energetic, but do you always fake your smiles?"

"When I'm on the clock, yes."

"Ouch."

"Everything about you makes me uncomfortable."

All joy melts out of him. "I deeply apologize. I always try to respect my employees and give no reason for my life to be used as the general public's entertainment. Despite that, we do find ourselves in close quarters often. If I've done anything—"

My eyes roll. "I'm not talking about *that*. I'm talking about *right now*. You're so…sickeningly sincere. With *everyone*. You tip. Always. Really well. At fast food restaurants. When there's terrible service. It doesn't matter.

You're just *kind* to everyone. And *another thing*, I've *never* entered a building behind you because you always open the door for me. When we split off on trips, you send one of your bodyguards with me to make sure I get to my room safe. The constant overbearing *joy* that leaks out of your pores is like a virus infecting everyone around you. You treat everyone with grace. You, as a person, barely seem real. But then add in your overflowing energy and childlike wonder?" Scoffing, I toss a hand at him. "You're *thirty-two*, Mr. Marsh. Why are you *always* moving? *How* are you always moving? Are you hooked up to caffeine twenty-four-seven?"

He stops twisting his chair.

"Is *tired* a state of being you even understand? Because the rest of us happen to exist in it. Perpetually." I huff, compose myself, make sure I'm maintaining my *customer service* voice. "All this to say, it's really not you. I'm just easily frustrated. I like when things make sense. And you don't. No one's supposed to be rich, handsome, and kind with no medical issues to speak of. The least you could do is have a mild case of asthma. *Come on.*"

"You're upset that I'm...too perfect?"

I scoff. Again. "I'm upset because it's my character. I'm upset because you carry yourself with the innocence of an idiot, but everything works out for you anyway. You're smart and respected even when you don't act like it. You work hard, but you don't have to *work hard* for much. I run on logic. You're fueled by emotion. We clash. And I pretend we don't because you pay well and I don't feel unsafe around you like I have at other assistant jobs." Heaving a sigh, I sweep my fingers through my short dark hair. "Can we *please* just pretend none of this happened?"

His gaze slips toward his computer screen, then down to the stack of papers in front of him. His fingers flex, and he shifts in his seat. "I'd…rather not."

"So I'm resigning?"

He lifts the stack of papers, offering it to me. "I'd prefer if you didn't."

"What's this?"

"My answers. To the form. And the list of questions I decided not to include. It's what you asked about for question 199. I didn't force myself to reach two hundred. I cut down from three-fourteen because I thought it was too long. Perhaps it wasn't actually long enough. After a single night, the form garnered hundreds of responses. Most of them useless. I came upon yours yesterday, and it struck me like none of the others had, so I've been preparing to confront you all night."

All night, he says. As though anyone who hasn't slept is allowed to look like him. He doesn't even have dark circles under his eyes. Without makeup, my bags could carry Saint Bernards.

"Consider it, please," he says. "Date me for a few months, then answer a yes or no question. If you still hate me too much to go through with marrying me, I won't force you. But if you humor me during this probationary period, I'll give you a Christmas bonus that covers your debt."

I go rigid, staring at him.

"In spite of my legal immunity, I'm happy to put that in writing if it would give you some security. I am also happy to issue a down payment constituting half of what you need to pay off your debts as I suspect having the cash in your account would provide further comfort."

He can't be serious. There has to be a catch. There's no way my answers to his questions warranted this kind of response. I'm missing the angle. The second I agree, he'll make my life terrible. He has to be interested in getting even. Humiliating me. Using me. *Something.*

Except, of course, that's what I'd do in his position. And we are very much night and day.

"Marcella..." he begins softly, "...you say we clash, but one of us spent hours tediously constructing a form in hopes of finding someone to spend their life with. The other spent hours filling it out. Genuinely. Whether you were passing the time or not, whether you were drunk or not, you can't tell me there wasn't any sincerity or thought put into your answers. You challenged every question from every direction, and it was stunning to behold." He moves the pages closer, urging me to grasp them. "In many ways, I think we're alike. Let me know what you think after you read my answers."

Hesitant, I take the stack. "Being somehow compatible on paper doesn't mean you don't completely annoy me in real life."

"Just consider it. Unless you were planning to quit on me before December, what do you have to lose?"

My dignity.

But wait.

I'm still hugging a trashcan, so I guess that ship has already sailed...

Chapter 2

See attached spreadsheet of pros and cons.

– Marcella

Brigid hums through my headphones while I slouch on my couch and whack bats in the mines of *Stardew Valley*—the best farming sim game ever made and my single solace. While the marriage candidates may be alcoholics or basement dwellers or sexist or immature or wannabes, they have never *once* posted an ad for a wife online.

I appreciate that.

Even though I shun them all in favor of having a cute sewer monster roommate every time.

Krobus, man.

That little guy gets me.

"I think you should do it," Penny says merrily.

"Let's not rush into this decision. There has to be a trick." Brigid sighs so loud the noise registers on our three-way Discord call. "Can someone harvest the greenhouse? I'm staying on the island another night."

"In the mines, beating up my feelings," I mutter, and smack a slime.

Penny chirps, "On it!"

"As I was saying—" Brigid starts.

"Do we have red cabbage?" Penny interrupts. "Jodi

wants one, and I think I can get it to her before I pass out."

That poor single mother is going to have a cabbage thrust in her face in the dead of night while she's in bed… Concerned Ape giving us a Key to the Town, which allows us to enter any home no matter the usual operating hours, is almost as hilarious as him letting us drink mayonnaise in the latest update. Most delightful dev ever, I swear.

I say, "I left one in my fridge."

"Got it!"

Brigid plows on as though we never cut into her deposition at all, "—there has to be some underlying reason Marsh is on the market for a wife. Did you ask why he needs one before Christmas, specifically?"

"I asked if he was going to lose a trust fund. He told me this wasn't a romcom."

Penny gasps. "That's not a *no*."

"Allowing his *no* to have any weight implies he wouldn't lie to you. He's a thriving business owner. He absolutely knows how to lie."

"Smart liars don't lie. Too much to keep track of." Penny giggles. "It's all about reading between the lines."

In the game, the clock in the top corner of my screen turns an angry red as we near pass out time, so I leave my monster-beating therapy to make a mad dash back to the farm. "I'm very bad at reading between the lines."

"We know," Brigid comments.

My already heinous slouch worsens when I pass out two feet from my in-game bed. "I have nothing but hate in my soul."

Penny giggles again. "We know that, too."

The corner of my mouth lifts. "So one vote yes, one vote no?" I'm supposed to be reviewing Mr. Marsh's list of answers tonight and really giving this some serious thought before tomorrow; however, the mines. They call to me. I yearn for them. And it's better to take such a decision before the council anyway.

"Oh, absolutely not *no*," Brigid says. "I've been organizing a list on my other monitor. Pros and cons, level of importance depicted through repeating points as necessary. If we assume he's being honest and there's no angle, this doesn't seem too bad no matter how you slice it. How large a sum of money are we talking just to go through with dating Marsh for a few months?"

"Ample," I mumble, and trot to my beloved in-game coffee machine. If I had automatic coffee each morning, real life conditions would improve drastically. Unfortunately, I can't actually afford coffee until Mr. Marsh lets me add one to the breakfast order he pays for.

Maybe that's a pro for him.

He provides me with the pennies required to feed myself each day.

"Should I designate three or five lines as 'money' on the pro side, in all caps?" Brigid asks.

"Is that the only pro?" I mumble and neglect to mention the coffee thing. Because I hate him and all that.

"Absolutely not."

"What's something else that's a pro?"

"Your boss is very hot."

I think I throw up a little of my fake coffee. Even though my little pixelated sprite character hasn't so much as drunk it yet. Wild.

"I love his hair. Can you put his pretty hair in the pro list, please?" Penny says as she, adorably, pops into my house and kitchen to offer me a rock. Penguin pebbling. Little, non-verbal *I love you's*. It's a gesture the three of us have had since we were all freshmen in high school, and I still have a bucket of non-virtual stones from Penny and Brigid in the corner of what would be my bedroom.

26

If I owned a bed.

"Is his pretty hair a valid pro, Marci? If you confirm that his attractiveness holds weight, I can list 'hot' five times, in all caps."

Penny's little avatar for this farm—a fully white in the hair and eyes disaster of a thing named "Smartfood" after the white cheddar popcorn—dances back and forth in front of me. "What do you say, Marciboo? Hot, rich husband, with pretty hair long enough to put tiny braids in. Many pros in that sentence. Many pros indeed."

"I think we're missing a pretty big point. He's spent the past two months with customer service me. And he only got the tiniest taste of real me this morning. I am not okay with marrying someone for their money and condemning myself to a lifetime of customer service."

"Real you is the you right now, right?" Penny asks. "Real you is a little shrimp on the couch, scowling at her screen, right?"

I blink, become aware of my face, and learn the momentary smile I experienced a few minutes ago is long gone. "Calling me a shrimp is not good for morale."

"Is it accurate, though?" Brigid asks.

I uncurl my spine and sit myself up, wiggling my chipped ladybug toes against the cushions as I stretch my back. "Not *anymore*."

"We stan a lass with good posture," Penny chirps. "The point is, we love the you that you are right now. He's interested at all because unhinged, drunk you wrote him an unhinged, drunk novella. Customer service you isn't the sarcastic mess that drunk you happens to be. He has to be smart enough to be interested in the real version of you, doesn't he? He obviously knows how to read people. Are you against giving him credit because you hate him and flinch at the notion he's seen any part of who you really

27

are?"

My nose scrunches, and I grab some extra Spicy Eels before marching myself out of my little farmhouse and to the mines again. "I dislike giving anyone credit for things they don't have to work for."

Brigid cuts in, "Okay, so let's say you take this offer and stop feeding him customer service Marci. You'll still have that down payment whenever he realizes you were right. As long as he's not malicious, you get an amicable breakup. And I really don't think he's malicious if he went through all the trouble of answering his own questions and printing them off for you. You don't lose, unless, of course, by the point of breakup it'll sting to have him tell you that he can't stand your character?"

"Oh, no. I'm totally used to people telling me that the second I'm comfortable enough to be myself around them. The issue here is that I am very much not eager to be myself around the bouncing, bubbling manchild."

"Is he really that immature? He always seems so pretty in pictures and interviews, which I watch, hoping I'll catch a glimpse of you being super adorable in the back with your little LeoPad." Penny joins me in the mines, gathering coal like a princess while I beat up all the Dust Sprites and protect her.

"I feed and dress him every day, while he smiles foolishly and never stops moving. He's a picky eater, too. I'm supposed to plan his meals around a nutrition guideline that would put public school lunch ladies to shame, and yet I'm still needing to adjust and adjust and adjust because he didn't provide me with a list of foods he doesn't like. And, sometimes, it isn't even the *food* he doesn't like. It's the combination. He sorts mixed vegetables, Penny. I once got him stir-fry noodles then watched him disassemble it for an hour during a Zoom call with his shareholders. Every leek, chicken, and broccoli was segregated into three distinct piles before he took a bite. A *cold* bite. And that wasn't okay, so he made me heat it up in three different frying pans. That I had to go out and buy and now keep in the break room to take with me whenever we travel anywhere." I rake in a breath, let it out slowly. A manic laugh leaves me. "If I were his wife, I'd end up killing one of us. Possibly both, him and then myself to avoid prison."

Brigid clears her throat. "*Wife* is already off the table. Completely off the table. That boy doesn't need a wife. He needs a live-in mother, and that is not going to be you." A pregnant pause slips into the static, and I don't like it. "However…three and a half months of giving it a chance… then going debt-free?"

"That doesn't sound so bad," Penny murmurs. "He's absolutely giving off little helpless puppy vibes, so not husband material, but also not unsafe."

"Leading him on for money is incredibly dishonest. Maintaining this relationship for three months at such a capacity that he doesn't break up with me before I get all the money I need to pay off my debts then saying *ha ha no* when he thinks I'm going to go through with marrying him is dishonest."

"Is it though?"

"Yes."

Brigid clears her throat. "But…*is it*? He kind of seems to like normal you, so maybe you don't have to pretend. He can't blame you if three months isn't enough time for you to accept a proposal. You've told him the truth. If he wants to take you on a few dates and find out for himself, you've been perfectly honest."

"Truly," Penny chimes in, "to not let him find out for himself insults his intelligence, which is unkind. Get the *told you so* moment, or get the full amount to pay off your debt. Either option sounds great to me."

I sag back into my couch cushions, realizing Penny and I have done just about an entire day in the mines. Except I've stopped moving forward, so she's just running circles around me beside a neglected ladder to the next cave level. Once I've returned to my true form as a shrimp, I mutter, "That is the most depressing *I told you so* I can think of. I *told* you I sucked and we wouldn't work out. I *told* you I was entirely disagreeable."

"You said that an affront against your character wouldn't bother you," Brigid reminds me.

"It wouldn't *bother* me. I'm just explaining that there is no joy to be found in this particular telling so."

"Fair."

"Do it!" Penny cheers. "Do it for me, please? Let me live vicariously through you. I've always wanted to date a rich man. I've been stuck with losers who have said *no* to dessert at restaurants a little too fast for a little too long. I am *dying* for a Coca-cola cake from Cracker Barrel and someone with enough spare change to get it for me." She sniffs. "I would simply go feral for that kind of man. Do you hear me? *Feral.*"

The bar is on the floor. It's embedded in the tile.

Why is my precious Penny dating the moles who would dig under it?

Brigid says, "As the happily married woman among us, I won't ask you to do it for me. I won't say that men aren't wholly disappointing sometimes, even when you do love and cherish them, unto death. I will just confirm that you have been perfectly honest with him, and you can continue to be because I sincerely can't think of an angle where this benefits him beyond accepting that he likes you for you. It's one autumn. Can you stomach one autumn in exchange for a lifetime of being debt-free?"

One autumn.

One autumn of crippling embarrassment.

One autumn of dropping the customer service façade and being my raw, sarcastic, disagreeable self for a man's perusal and judgment.

One exhausting, dreadful autumn.

"Fine," I mutter. "I'll talk to him tomorrow during lunch."

Riveting spreadsheet. Are you aware I can access the edit history? You deleted HOT fourteen times.

– Finnegan

Chapter 3

I regret this already.

– Marcella

Penny: AHHHHHHHHH. I HATE YOU.

I smile at my phone as Penny's texts come in.

Penny: Please marry ME. Forget about your boss. You deserve the housewife, bb girl.

Penny: I cook. I clean. I provide ROCKS. Full pakidge, right here.

Making my way back inside after getting Mr. Marsh's and my lunch from the delivery guy at the front of the building, I fit myself into a cramped elevator and watch a stream of images appear on my phone. Penny's big green eyes and short curly blond hair make her look like a professional model—regardless of the fact she's doing a romantic spoof with the Coca-cola cake I DoorDashed to her on company time.

Penny: Would it be weird if I start making out with this cake? It's still warm. I'm sobbing. Why are you the best? Marsh needs to fall in love with you during these next few months, or else I'm throwing hands.

Adjusting my food bag, I reply:

Marcella: That's not a good ending. I don't want to turn down a simpering puppy dog guy who will then have to let me go on account of it being too difficult to work with me. I want one date to end with: "Wow, this was an expensive realization, oops, see you tomorrow with my coffee and schedule."

Penny: But then you won't get all your debt paid off.

Marcella: Fine. I want him to tolerate me for a few months and be too stubborn to admit he was wrong before he accepts that he made an expensive mistake.

Penny: Fair enough. Sadly, you are much too lovable. Make sure he, in all his love-struck can't-bear-to-be-around-you-and-not-kissing-ness, writes you the best recommendation letter ever. Get him to hook you up with a female CEO. They probably don't come with this drama.

Sadly, they also don't come with this pay.

I guess I forgot to consider that no matter what happens, I'm toying with a difficult balance if I agree to this. If he dislikes the real me way too much, I may be able to pay off half my debts, but he may fire me. If he likes the real me too much for some lunatic reason, I might still be forced to give up this position if I don't go through with whatever he will want from me after the dating period is over.

I need to crunch these numbers before I confirm or deny this insanity…

And I don't have much time before this elevator empties, leaving just me on Mr. Marsh's top floor.

Getting a job that pays this well was pure happenstance. Even if I don't get a bulk sum now, I'll be able to pay off my debts with this salary, right?

Probably the college one…

The other, though?

The other isn't exactly on the up and up. It's a loan I took out when I was in college full time and Dad had to have an emergency surgery for cancer, followed by treatment. I panicked when Mom called me, sobbing and saying we couldn't afford it.

The amount we needed was a blur of numbers with too many zeros.

And the consequence of not paying that outrageous amount would have been losing my father.

No one was accepting my parents' credit score.

So I made a skeezy deal with interest rates through the roof, no clear record amounts, and a bill every month that seems to *only* cover interest. Even paying monthly thousands, I still owe tens of thousands. And the only way I have a chance of getting rid of it is if I drop the kind of money Mr. Marsh is offering all at once at their business front with witnesses. I need proof of an *all clear* and to get out of there once and for all.

Even if Mr. Marsh doesn't keep me through the full three-month term, having half of what I need gives me a head start that will take years off this battle. I have to do this. At least part way.

I have to take the risk and accept.

Taking a deep breath, I swap my phone for my LeoPad once I reach my desk right outside Mr. Marsh's office.

Just…be honest.

I'm great at being direct.

It's why so few kids liked me growing up.

It's a real…a real super power.

Yeah.

I dare say I might need my trashcan again before this is done.

All the same, I tuck my LeoPad under the arm holding Mr. Marsh's lunch and knock.

"Come on in," he calls, so I push through into the blinding space.

With the full wall of glass windows overlooking the

city dead ahead, sunlight fills every crevice inside, bouncing off the ivory whites and ash grays. It's crisp. Clean. Clinical. I'd appreciate the décor if it weren't for the waterfall feature ending in an entire koi pond on the left across from Mr. Marsh's desk. Having five live fish the size of my head swimming in your office flooring is where I, quite honestly, draw the line on whimsical.

It takes everything in me to remain calm, cool, and collected as I deliver Mr. Marsh's meal while second-guessing my opening line for this conversation. I've been editing it all morning. It still seems to suck.

Before I get the nerve to broach the subject, he says, "You don't have to force a smile around me. I wanted to tell you that when we were reviewing today's schedule this morning, but it was a time crunch with that early meeting."

My entire script burns to a crisp, and I'm stuck smiling and staring as my brain struggles to reload.

The urge to put my fist through his face then eat his chicken parm is *so* high right now.

I'm a saint.

I'm actually a saint.

Every day, I stop murders with my impeccable self control.

As eloquent as a slug, I say, "That's not…really how it works. You get business mode, and you don't want me to turn off business mode during business hours because I will one hundred percent cuss out your clients if they get on my nerves."

His blue eyes sparkle as he tilts his head. All I can see is a giant puppy when he says, "Do they do that often? Get on your nerves?"

"Constantly. You know how the human body has trillions and trillions of nerves?"

"Yes?"

35

"I keep mine on the floor in a puddle around my ankles. If anyone gets within three feet of me, I guarantee they're on a couple billion of my nerves. The skill it takes to pretend they aren't is actually quite commendable. I deserve an Oscar."

An amused edge softens the bliss in his usual smile. "Fascinating."

I swallow hard as I take a breath. "Mr. Marsh. I've given your proposition some thought."

"Did you read my answers to the form questions?"

I...skimmed some, then I got overwhelmed and called my girls to see if they wanted to play *Stardew Valley*. But I shan't be saying that, I think. "I started; however, the task did not fit into my plans for the evening." I'm not getting paid to learn your favorite color, my guy. I do not have the capacity to care. "My motivation for what I'm about to say is purely monetary. I believe fully that you'll have had enough of me after one date. If you're willing to pay for that, I'll consent to it."

"You'll consent to one date? Or you'll consent to the full term?" He twists his chair. "I'm only interested in a full-term chance."

"I believe you'll be done after one date. I'm not consenting to a full term without more details concerning expectations. How many dates do you anticipate during the period? Must I emotionally prepare for casual texts? Phone calls? How much of my free time will you expect me to give up, assuming you stay interested through November? I want a contract."

"Funny." He stops twisting to pull out a formal document. Placing it perfectly at the edge of the desk in front of me, he says, "Does this outline everything of consequence?"

With a mere glance, no. Absolutely not. "What does my

agreeing to treat this like a real dating relationship mean?" It's the vaguest garbage I have ever seen. "I want hours. Events. The number of times I'm required to text back in a given day."

"Marcella."

Brow furrowed, I look up, and I fear my calm, cool, collected smile has gone disgustedly lopsided.

He seems much too chipper for my liking when he gently prods, "I want to test out a relationship. I already know you're an excellent employee, but I'm not offering you another job. I'm asking you to treat me like your boyfriend for a few months. That means texting back when you would, going on dates when you would, being yourself under the condition that you treat me like your boyfriend. You have full autonomy to accept or decline my requests and advances if they do not interest you, knowing I will respect your wishes as I would respect someone I am emotionally-invested in."

I tense. "So. No hard guidelines? No relationship agreement? No rules?" I forget I'm still operating during business hours and scoff. "Don't be ridiculous. Relationships come with terms. And many of them fall apart because those terms aren't ever solidified in text. I'll paint you a picture: Joe and Sue are married. Joe and Sue have a verbal arrangement where Sue does the cooking and the laundry while Joe does the dishes and works. One day, Joe is too tired to do the dishes. This infuriates Sue, which infuriates Joe. Things devolve into a he said, she said, and neither person feels like the other cares about them, so they get divorced. How could poor Joe and Sue have avoided this tragic outcome? Well, easy. If they'd had a physical agreement to refer to with a clause concerning shared housework, they might have had the sense to build in a procedure for human error. They could have made a chart together and decided on the allotted number of graces in a given month for those times when Sue couldn't bear to cook and Joe couldn't stomach the dishes. Instead, they're sad and alone and now *both* of them are working and cooking and cleaning up all by themselves. *The end.*" My voice pitches by mistake, so I reel myself in and bite my tongue.

Watching me as though I'm the most interesting little lump in the world, Mr. Marsh asks, "Are your parents divorced?"

"Happily married and going on thirty years, why?"

"So they have a relationship agreement?"

"No. They're just really good people, and they love each other, so both of them are always trying to do both the cooking and the cleaning for the other. It's very cute, honestly." My arms fold. "I am nowhere near as good, loving, or cute. If we agreed that your job was to do the dishes, and you didn't do them one day, I'd stab you with a dirty knife, and you'd get an infection, and as you were dying, I'd whisper above your bedside, *this wouldn't have happened if it were* clean."

Mr. Marsh slaps a hand to his mouth before he crumples, gripping the edge of his desk for dear life. Hissing breaths whistle from his nose as he battles to pull himself together. It is a lost cause. His chest shakes with silent laughter, and he can barely crack one eye to look at me. "That mental image is my favorite thing."

I reclaim composure, tilt my LeoPad forward, and direct my attention at the screen. "Shall I contact an artist to commission it for you, sir?"

He swears. "Yes. Please. I'd like an entire comic. Hire a small business. Whatever price they ask, double, no, *triple* it."

I pull my gaze off my reflection in the black screen to

meet his eyes. "I was being sarcastic." I turn the dark screen toward him. "This isn't even on."

"Oh. Well. I'm not being sarcastic. Also, I think your tone is supposed to change when you're being sarcastic."

My lips purse. Yeah. So they tell me. "Sir, the point is, I don't feel comfortable entering into this without more stable expectations."

He fills his big chest with air, releases it, leans back, *twists*. "Fine. You drive a hard bargain, pumpkin."

Every last nerve in my puddle electrifies, standing on end. Revolt soars through my chest. And I cannot be held responsible for the state of my face in response to his calling me *pumpkin*.

Merrily, he continues, "I'll pay everything up front and cover all costs associated with this *if* you treat me like your boyfriend for the period leading up to November 30, when I expect your answer at the altar."

My mouth is dry.

Everything? Up front. I can get rid of my debt in a matter of days? Start putting my paycheck into things like…like a truly functional AC? I could start looking for a nicer apartment. In a matter of *weeks*, I could move somewhere without loud neighbors?

I could afford to order another cake to celebrate?

I could *buy a bed*?

"Treat you like my boyfriend?" I whisper.

"That's right. No relationship agreements. Just genuine communication and healthy boundaries. The free will to accept or decline my invitations to go out without worrying that you need to stick to a strict set of regulations."

I feel ill. Completely ill. The sensation rides up the back of my throat and swirls in my stomach. "Mr. Marsh—"

"Also, I will need you to call me by an endearment for the duration of this test. I'll allow grace for *Finn*, but never

39

Mr. Marsh and absolutely not *sir.*"

I am going to die. Say *his first name*? To his *face*? What kind of person does he think I am? A temptress? A promiscuous, brazen, forward lass? Does he assume I walk around showing my *ankles* to just anyone?

Using a man's first name in a romantic setting is just about the same heat level as making out.

With. Tongue.

I suppose I'm just never going to refer to him ever again.

His lunch is getting cold. My lunch is getting cold. He has another appointment after lunch. Actually, he has seven back-to-back appointments after lunch. Where does he even get the time to be such a clown?

My head hurts.

I desperately want to be able to afford another cake from Publix. It's all I've ever dreamed of, really. Mouth dry, I say, "You realize if I agree to this, I'm agreeing to money? You'll have wasted a lot of money on someone you probably won't like very quickly, on someone whose motivation behind being around you is purely *money.*"

"Yes, I realize that."

"You want a gold digger for a wife?"

He rises, slowly towering over his desk—and me. I've never accepted that he's an entire head taller. It's cruel to have to look up into his ever-present sunshine smile when I'm little more than a pitiful rain cloud, just trying to make a living by diffusing some of his rays. "May I touch you briefly?" he asks.

I try to wet my lips. "Where?"

"Chin."

I grimace and clutch my LeoPad as I murmur, "If you must."

Warm, his hand cups my face, fixing my attention on

his sculpted cheekbones, his gentle eyes, the strong lines of his jaw, those super gentle eyes, both of them cheekbones again, an ear, another ear.

He chuckles. "Pick one place to look, pumpkin. Your eyes are very distracting jumping around like that."

I settle on his nose to keep my thoughts off the fact having him touch me is such an unpleasant sensation. His nose is large, but not too large. Straight. It doesn't look like it's ever been broken before. There's not a single bump to speak of. One week with me as a "girlfriend," and I might be inclined to fix that...

Once I've settled, he says, "You are honest, hardworking, intuitive, and—as I'm discovering—genuine when you let yourself be. I don't need you to be kind or caring. I don't want a woman to coddle or pamper me. I want a companion who's less superficial than many of the people I find myself surrounded by. I want someone who makes me laugh. For hours. At nearly every one of her two hundred blatant, unfiltered answers. I'd like someone like you. And you, Marcella, couldn't be a gold digger if you tried." His lips quirk as his thumb swipes my cheek, making my skin crawl. "I think we both know you'd be coming for my kidneys before you come for a penny beyond what covers your debt."

He is not wrong.

But I am not prepared to suggest he is right.

"Do we have an agreement?" he asks.

Thoughts distant, I say, "Three and a half months. Until a wedding November 30?"

He nods. "Where you will say I do, or I don't."

"Publicly?"

"I'm not a monster."

"That is the answer to a different question."

"I will be editing these terms for you before the end of

41

the day, and I will specify that your decision not be made in public. But, it will be made the day of the wedding, when everything is already planned, set up, and paid for. It will be made in a back room on-site of whatever venue we choose. And you will be in a wedding gown when you make it."

I hiss a swear. "How about I just text you a gif that says *eff no* the morning of November 30?"

He bites his lip in an effort to subdue his smile. "I find my wishes to be extremely reasonable."

"*Reasonable?* You're going to waste so much money on a wedding."

"For someone who calls herself a gold digger, you are very concerned about my finances. Half a million dollars is the cost of a luxury wedding. Do you know how many *millions* are in a singular billion?"

"I try not to think about your net worth because it makes me question the ethics of your existence."

"Do you know how many companies a luxury wedding would benefit? We can source all décor and guest favors from private owners. I'm thinking hundreds of jobs for hundreds of people. And then, after we're married, you'll have a special credit card. So much spending money. You can distribute the wealth to anyone you want."

"Aren't you getting ahead of—"

He lays a finger against my lips—even though he absolutely didn't ask to touch me there, and it makes me slightly murderous. "Reminding you that marrying me doesn't mean *husband and wife* things if that's not what you want. In a few months, you might not hate me anymore. Then we can be amicable companions."

I swat his hand away. "This sounds like you're paying for a lifelong friend. That's really sad. I'm sad for you."

"Do we have an agreement?"

Closing my eyes, I take a firm step back, out of his reach, square my shoulders, and say, "I expect the contract on my desk in plain language as soon as possible. Include a clause that relieves me of all liability and refund if you cancel this foolishness midway. Also, as we'll be officially dating—" It takes everything in me not to gag. "—starting tomorrow, you should organize to have a gift prepared for me in the morning. A celebration token, if you will. Lastly, the code word is *pickles*."

His head lolls, bright eyes filling with confusion. "Code word? Like...a safe word? What sorts of things do you expect of your significant others if you start your relationships with a safe word?"

I narrow my eyes. "If you *want* to call it a *safe word*, be my guest. It does, in fact, keep you *safe*. As in, if I say it, get as far away from me as is physically possible. Or else I cannot be held responsible for the consequences."

With that, I turn on my heel and leave his office to find my soggy, sweating foam container of pasta for lunch on my desk.

In some ways, it feels like an omen.

Pity, I've never been one to believe in superstitions.

Chapter 4

This is why smart people don't have *fish tanks* for *floors.*

– Marcella

"Thanks. I hate it." I puff a breath out of my nose the second the contents of the jewelry box Mr. M...my *temporary significant other* is holding open for me register.

It is a necklace.

With a tiny gold pumpkin charm.

The delicate outline and the subtle glitter of the tiny diamonds embedded in the gold is thoroughly beautiful. I am appalled to say I do *not* actually hate it. I simply hate what it means, what it stands for, the entire emotional reasoning behind it...

Oh yeah.

And the person holding it.

I should have been more specific yesterday.

See, by *gift* I meant *food*, so I could drown my feelings in something more tolerable than this situation. Like a chocolate parfait.

Clearly, I'm not the only one who sucks at reading other people's minds.

Fi...the *guy's* eyes brighten. "You're not faking a smile this morning. Should I warn my clients and any visitors to maintain a ten-foot clearance?"

"For their own safety, absolutely." Setting a hand to my chest, I force a sardonic smirk. "Congratulations. I was thinking about it last night, and I decided that for the sake of this little experiment of yours, it's only fair if I fully downgrade you from my *assistant* package to my *girlfriend* package."

"Downgrade?" he echoes.

"Don't worry. My work won't suffer, but you might. On account of my attitude." Throwing together my best grin, I chirp, "Please remember, upgrading is free."

"No, no. This is the upgrade." Snapping the box shut, and opening it again, and snapping it shut, and opening it again, he leans back against his desk. "Your voice is so much lower than I'm used to."

"In order to survive in professional settings, many women adopt a persona that feeds into the feminine expectation. Pleasant smiles. Lilting tone." I drop my attention to my tablet, wake it up, and open Ffff...my *dearly beloved* boyfriend's schedule. "You have a seven o'clock breakfast at—"

"May I take you out this evening?" *Snap. Snap. Snap.* "If I have dinner plans, cancel them."

"No, it's a work night. Also, it's Wednesday, which means you do have dinner plans. With your mother. I'm off the clock early."

"That's right. It is Wednesday, isn't it?" *Snap. Snap. Snap.* "You could come with me. Meet my mother."

"Respectfully, that is never a first date activity."

Snap.

I grab his hand, crushing his fingers and the box. Meeting his eyes, I hiss, "I will kill you in your sleep if you don't stop this."

"You are such an affectionate girlfriend." He drops his head an entire foot so his forehead bonks into mine. "It's

45

only been one day, yet you want to be with me while I'm asleep?"

Heat rushes up my neck.

"*Rrr-ow.*"

And it plummets—like nausea—into my stomach, which falls promptly to my toes. "Never do that again."

"Might I do the proper *boyfriend* thing and put the necklace on you?"

My eyes narrow. I'm waiting for the cash he sent me to clear in my account, but it is incoming. He's paying a lot of money for a girlfriend experience. Which was one hundred percent a terrible financial decision on his part, yet I'm the one stuck feeling mildly guilt-ridden.

Sighing, I step back, turn, and tilt my head forward to pull my short hair fully off my neck. "Do you need me for your seven o'clock, or should I stay here and sort through emails?"

"You can sort through emails on your pad while I get you breakfast." His arms come around me, and the tiny pumpkin falls against my chest.

For some inexplicable reason, my heart rate kicks up. "I think I'd prefer to stay here and starve."

The chain touches my throat. "Unfiltered Marcella is my favorite thing. Have you been internally this hateful for the past two months?"

"Ye—" His fingers fiddle with the clasp, tickling cold metal against me.

I jerk forward, choke myself for a second, then watch the tiny pumpkin charm fly across the room.

Straight into the koi pond.

My mouth drops open.

"Are you all right?" he who shall not be named asks me.

My shoulders bunch as I ease around, find the loose

chain dangling from his fingers. "I'm so sorry," I exhale. "I...I didn't mean to do that." I fight down a swallow. "H-how much did that cost?"

His eyes widen before an unnerving smile curls his lips. "Only a couple hundred. Don't worry about it."

"A couple *hundred*," I choke. "Do you know how many Publix cakes you could get with that? *Several* small ones. *And like two big ones*."

"That sounds like tomorrow's gift idea."

"Don't you *dare* get me a gift every day." I throw a finger toward the koi pond. "*Clearly*, I am a *hazard*, and I cannot be trusted around *nice things*."

His hand lifts and lands atop my head. My eye twitches as he pats. If I weren't in shock, the weight of his gentle pat-patting would make me violent. "Don't worry about it, pumpkin. I got it off Etsy. Small seller. They were more than happy to rush order it and let one of my employees pick it up to fly here on a private jet. I'll just request another one and have it replaced by the weekend."

"No. I do not need it that badly. At all, actually."

"You're being a bad gold digger again."

"I'm being an exemplary girlfriend. You should be honored." What am I saying?

He chuckles. "I am." Lifting a finger, he touches his neck. "Per chance are you sensitive around here?"

"Maybe," I snap. *Maybe* I'm sensitive around *everywhere*. And *maybe* that's why my parents tell me I used to hit kids for touching me when I was growing up.

"Can't stand tight shirts or turtlenecks?" he prompts.

"Turtlenecks are knitted in hell, by the devil. Change my mind."

"Can't. I agree."

"You're going to be late for your breakfast. I'm staying here to sort through emails and wallow in self-loathing."

47

He bites his lip. "An excellent pastime. I look forward to a report on how it went when I return, with some takeout for you. Are pancakes okay?"

My eyes roll. "Yeah, sure."

He meanders to the door, sets his hand on the knob, and glances at me over his shoulder. "Also. Don't go swimming while I'm gone. I can and will just order another one. So please don't worry about it. I mean it."

I throw him the finger, wait for the door to close behind him, then take off my stupid blazer.

Chapter 5

Some things can't be bought.

– Finnegan

"November 30th…" my mother murmurs as she looks at the picture of Marcella on my phone. My little pumpkin's scowl and rolling eyes are too cute for words. With her scrunched nose and crossed arms, she looks livid, but the tiny gold necklace resting against her chest tells me everything I need to know about her character.

When I insisted on taking this picture several hours ago, she smelled like fish.

"She's very pretty." My mother smiles, returning my phone. "Why haven't I heard about her before? November is so soon for a wedding. And you're very important. Are you sure she isn't after your money, Finny?"

My chest pinches, but I keep smiling. "I'm sure. She's very low maintenance."

My mother's thin white brows rise. "Really? She was dressed so nicely."

"She takes care of herself." Absolutely wouldn't spend thirty minutes skipping breakfast to search through pebbles in a koi pond for a tiny pumpkin charm she hates. No, no, no. Couldn't be her. *Wouldn't* be her, rather. Certainly not. "I wanted you to meet her tonight, but something came up."

My mother's small frame droops as she eases back against the floral print sofa in her modest home where I maintain a full staff that sees to everything she needs. Given her accelerating condition, keeping everything close is…safer. "Pity." Her lips pout. "Does she not like me?"

"What?" I pocket my phone and tut. "Don't be silly. She's just a little shy."

"Shy," my mother repeats. Her mind drifts, and it takes everything in me to wait out the ripple, knowing in a moment this entire conversation will be gone. When her attention refocuses on me, her smile spears me through the chest. "Finny, do you know when your father will be home? I'd like to try a new casserole tonight. I hope he likes it."

It hurts to swallow.

Dad's been dead for years. And Mom hasn't been able to cook for…

Well.

I'd really rather not think about the last time I had a home-cooked meal of my mother's.

"Why don't you tell me about the last casserole Dad loved? What was it again…peanut butter carrot loaf?"

She laughs. "No, *no*. We *all* hated that. What a disaster." As she drifts into the story of the infamous—and utterly terrible—creation, I find myself piecing her words together before she finds them. I weave them in my head until they're full pictures that I can copy and keep. Forever.

Somewhere in the back of my mind, doctor visits and test results and projections plague me. Somewhere in the back of my mind, *she may make it to January, but December is more realistic* crushes the breath from my lungs.

Once she's gone, I'll have no family left.

Even now, just the idea of that loneliness leaves me feeling bitterly cold before fall has had any chance to change over the seasons. I will be alone in winter. Possibly alone for Christmas. No one I'm close with isn't linked to *the business*. No parties or events or breakfasts, lunches, dinners I have aren't *networking*.

All throughout my childhood and into inheriting my father's industry, it's been hard to find people without ulterior motives. When having a cold warrants news coverage, it's hard to put faith in friends, never knowing when they might turn their backs on me and use personal information as their next publicity stunt. Being at the top of the world means being in a constant spotlight with constant surveillance. Trust is a commodity in short supply.

But, then again, so are women who would sift through a koi pond for a cheap piece of jewelry.

One way or another, it will be okay.

I will be okay.

Even if all the money in the world can't buy me more time.

Chapter 6

What part of <u>struggles with change</u> did you not understand?

– Marcella

"Fi…" Squinting in my bathroom mirror, I death-stare at the shape of my mouth as it wraps around the first two letters of my *dear, dear* boyfriend's name. I'm all but biting my lip. Like he does periodically. What a narcissistic name if it makes everyone pick up that bad habit of his.

My lips pull back from my teeth as I achieve the *N* sound.

The dim yellow glow of my bathroom light makes my harsh expression and flushed, fresh-from-a-hot-shower skin look ghastly.

Honestly.

What is that man thinking?

"All together now," I mutter. "Fff…" I swear instead.

Dropping my head, I stare at the off-white sink. It's crammed right next to my toilet, which is smooshed right against a standing shower. It's a straight, unflattering line of plumbing appliances with a half foot of dingy linoleum in front of it.

I need to look for apartments with bathrooms that don't cosplay as closets.

I need to locate the main office of that stupid loan

company. By the time my September bill is due, I have to be on their doorstep.

In less than two weeks, their stupid scam ends and my money will be my own. So by around mid-September, I want to be out of here, in a place with a bathtub, lighting that doesn't make me look like a horror movie character, and enough room in front of my toilet to take a deep breath without hitting the toilet paper holder.

My ambitions might just be a little out of control.

Eye twitching, I try an endearment on for size— something classic, emotionless. "Honey."

Suddenly, I'm in a sitcom from the 1960's, playing a little wife. And I swear to all that is good that is the last thing I want the F-meister to picture. Seeing me as his *little wife* is what we are trying to avoid. Thank you very much.

Why in the world did I fill out that dumb form?

Because, Marcella, if you hadn't, you wouldn't be paying off a debt with over a hundred percent interest next month. Because, Marcella, if you *hadn't*, you wouldn't be giving up on finding a nickname for your idiotic boss in favor of looking into *nice* apartments instead.

Defeated, I drag myself out of the bathroom, get changed into my pj's, and curl up on my couch with my laptop. Without five thousand dollars going to loans every month...I could get a stupid nice place. Is that...is that really true? *What?*

Sitting up straighter, I drag a leg against my chest and scroll through the options within my post-debt budget. Multiple bedrooms. Multiple bathrooms. These pictures look like they belong in magazines. These places have built-in heating and air. From actual vents. In the ceiling.

No. I'm totally delusional. There's no way I can afford this kind of stuff. Let's pop out a handy-dandy calculator and go through my finances one more time. With *feeling*.

...

I could buy a house.

An actual house.

If I stick it out in this crappy apartment until the new year, I'll have enough money to get a down payment on a modest house with a mortgage low enough for me to afford a Publix cake *every week*. Which is, of course, a terrible plan unless I am also planning to become quite *rotund* in a vastly unhealthy manner, but you know something else?

I could afford a gym membership.

A quick, hopeful Google search informs me that, no, exercise doesn't negate the effects of an unhealthy diet, so I'm glaring at my screen when my phone begins to ring. Without glancing too hard at where I have it set beside my laptop, I slide the FaceTime answer scroll.

"Hey, if you're Brigid, leave your husband and move into a mansion with Penny and me. If you're Penny, we're moving into a mansion together. Help me convince Bridge to leave her husband."

A distinctly *low* throat clear alerts me that I am talking to neither Penny nor Brigid. My attention flies toward my screen, which contains a face. A masculine face. A Ffff... face.

Thanks to all my good practicing, I swear, grab the loose neck of my pajama t-shirt—which contains roughly fifty holes from where the washed-to-death fabric has started to give up—and scoot back, frantic. I am *only* in a ratty t-shirt and a pair of underwear. And...and my camera is pointed at my ceiling.

Thank goodness my camera is pointed at my ceiling.

"I don't believe I'm either of the people you expected," Flibbertigibbets says, somewhat distractedly.

"Why are you *video calling me* at—" My attention flies to the corner of my computer screen. "—seven-thirty at night?"

Frogbutt's blue eyes turn weepy. "Because. I've texted and audio called for work-related things this late before. This call isn't work-related. I needed a distinction."

Oh. A distinction. I get it. That makes perfect sense. No big deal. It's just… Well… *Now I need heart medication.*

I'm sitting here half naked because he wanted to distinguish that this wasn't a work call where he'd be telling me to pack my bags and be at the airport in thirty minutes. I am going to *cut* him in the morning. "Calling me on video this late is extremely inappropriate behavior for the first *day* of a new relationship."

"It isn't even past dusk, Marcella."

"I *always* run on *winter* time. So it is well past dusk and, in fact, nearly my bedtime. I must be asleep by eight, lest the shadows activate my seasonal depression."

He ignores me to comment, "Is that water damage on your ceiling?"

I balk, scoff, reel. "*Excuse* you! Do *not* come into my *home* and judge my *ceiling.*"

Something distinctly breaks downstairs, shattering like a bomb going off. In seconds, the least-functional relationship in the world is screaming swears at each other, while more stuff breaks.

No small amount of distress wanders into Frankfurt McGee's weepy blue eyes.

"Shut up," I hiss. "Don't you even—"

"Where are you right now?" He's standing. I dislike this. Very much.

"You sit back down. You sit back down *right now.*"

"Your friend, Brigid, is she in an abusive relationship?"

I blurt, "What?"

The camera angle shifts, and I think this man is pulling on his shoes. "I'm attempting to emotionally manipulate you, full disclosure. You mentioned convincing her to leave her husband and move into a mansion with you and… Penny, was it?"

"Do not desecrate my friends' names in my own abode, sir."

He comes back into view, brows dipped with disappointment. "What did I tell you about calling me *sir*?"

"It's the *internet* sir, dang it! Note the absence of respect in my tone."

He frowns. Actually frowns. I don't know that I've ever seen him frown before. Never once. It's…not a bad expression on him, truly. "Where do you live, Marcella?"

I wish I had a gun. Georgia is a *Stand Your Ground* state. Thus, lethal force is allowed to prevent things like home invasion. As a wee lassie in my underwear, being preyed upon by Frickerfracker here, if he shows up at my door, I totally have a valid reason to shoot him.

I just, still, don't have pants.

And Fuzznugget is smart enough to remember he's my boss and has my address on file any second now.

Before I can scramble for my closet, I learn that *someone* has a gun downstairs.

The second a shot fires, my skin goes cold, and I spit out my address as though I'm fully clothed, as though *my dearest sweetest boyfriend* will save me.

I am wearing pants when the cops show up outside my windows, casting red and blue lights into the dying sun rays. I am wearing pants when F-boy—no do *not* call him that—shows up outside my door, flanked by my two favorite bodyguards in all black.

He's past my archway in a second, cupping my cheek firmly and scanning me from head to toe. It's force I'm

56

unused to and unsure whether or not I like, but the palpable worry pouring off him keeps me quiet. A relieved breath leaves his chest once he's identified that I'm still alive, I guess.

When his attention skims my living room, sheer bewilderment breeds with the worry, twisting his expression into a minefield of concern. "Marcella...you live...*here*?" Starkly horrified, he covers his mouth. "I thought I paid you well. The economy can't be *this* bad."

I do not want to tell him that my debt is actually somewhat insurmountable if he hasn't figured that part out yet, so I cross my arms and mutter, "Actually, it *can* be. Look in my bedroom. I don't even own a bed. It's just a gaping floor space, whereby I partake of the occasional existential crisis."

Perhaps he missed the sarcasm in my tone, because F-man—somehow, this works for my brain—sets me gently aside and *marches* to my room. A half-strangled gasping sound of mutilated despair echoes up my hallway as I fix my usual composed calm into place and tilt my head up at F-man's massive guards.

"Jeff, Mark, doing well?"

Jeff smiles while Mark shrugs his giant, tattooed arms and grunts a *so-so* sort of reply.

F-man stomps back up my hallway, a hand with a pointing finger thrown out behind him. "*There's no bed in there!*"

I drop my cheap smile. "I did *say* so."

"You got the sarcastic tone right that time. I thought you were *joking*. Where do you *sleep*?"

I jab my thumb at my couch. The simple throw blanket over the armrest nearest the coughing AC window unit is probably nicely chilled by now, meaning it's just about bedtime. Shame that I have *unexpected company*.

"Sometimes," I begin, wistful, "I pretend I'm a little homeless lass, curled up on one of those sofas country folk leave on their front lawns for weeks on end with a water-damaged *FREE* sign taped to the back cushions…"

All the peachy red undertones in F-man's skin drain away, leaving his hair more orange than usual. "Marcella…"

"You know something?" I say, taking a step closer to him.

"I'm not sure I want to…"

The corner of my mouth tips up. "You're more palatable when you aren't smiling all the time."

His throat bobs as red soars back up his neck. Softly, he says, "You aren't the only one with a dedicated work persona, pumpkin."

My nose wrinkles. "You ruined this moment with that nickname. This plot point is over. I'm going to couch now. Goodbye."

His eyes widen a fraction, then his shaken concern melts into a gentle smile as he bites his bottom lip. "I hope you know I'm never letting you sleep here again."

"I hope you aren't suggesting you'll make choices that would separate me from my emotional-support black mold. I think my lungs have grown dependent on it."

His smile vanishes, and he frees his lip. Yippee. He says, "Surely now you're joking."

I show him under my kitchen sink and the wall above the shower. When he's the silly, sad outline of a man who appears to have lost all sense of self, I say, "I'm planning to move out either mid-September or early next year. I'm just trying to decide whether I want a better apartment or if I want to house hunt. With how often you spring surprise trips on me, I need to craft a secure haven for my days and nights of blissful recharge. Having a house, somewhere that's *mine*, may assist in those dreams. I have always wanted a butterfly garden, so I'll need a yard."

"Done," he says.

I blink.

"*Already* done."

My eyebrow arches.

Grasping my shoulders, he takes a deep breath. "I have a house ten minutes out of the city. It's yours now. Bring Penny. Save Brigid. If she requires legal assistance, my lawyers will be in touch tomorrow morning. You'll wake up to fresh coffee and a Publix cake. There's staff, security, *and* a thriving butterfly garden. The centerpiece fountain that lights up is the only light around for fifty acres. You'll be able to see the stars."

I stare at this crazy, crazy man who seems to have decided my pukingly-content-to-be-married friend is in a toxic relationship. Sure, I joke that she should divorce her husband every other day because Cody is a *monster* who doesn't like *snakes*, but that's just, like, normal friend stuff.

No boy would be perfect enough for the goddesses that are my best friends. Period.

Freeing my shoulders from F-man's grasp, I cough, soaking in the awkward vibes, probably because Jeff and Mark are lingering threateningly in my living room right now. You know. Within earshot and whatever. "You're getting a little carried away and a little ahead of yourself, don't you think?"

"There are police lights outside your window. Right this second."

"That's called *ambiance*."

His eyes close. He spreads his fingers and takes a calming, long inhale. I hope it fills his rich chest with black mold. When his eyes open again, he's doing that *bright smile* thing I abhor with every cell in me. "Pumpkin, I am so pro healthy relationship. I *love* communication. I'm very invested in treasuring, respecting, and upholding your opinions, values, and decisions. I want to cherish everything you care about and prove that I also care. Your body, your mind, *precious*. Your spirit, angelic. Your soul, invaluable. It is my honor to protect you and your peace in every way by employing kindness and consideration at every possible intersection. *No* means *no*."

"Yawn. Can you get to the point before I throw up?"

"The *point* is, I am not fond of force, but you are *absolutely* never going to sleep here again. You are going to get in your car with your necessities, and I am going to escort you personally to my vacation home. Tomorrow, we'll work on saving and moving in your friends."

Without smiling, I let a deranged few laughs fall from my lips. "You're misunderstanding. Brigid is fine, living a fairy tale, and Penny and I don't live together because she's like you—bright and bubbly and *loud*. I love her to death in every possible way, but she listens to music in her bedroom. Without headphones. I'd simply kill her. And then myself. Because I don't want to picture a world without her."

"You have very complicated feelings."

"Thanks. I think it's called *being a person*. Not a fan, honestly. But here we are."

Combing his fingers through his hair, he says, "It'll be fine. The house is thirty-thousand square feet. You can have opposite side bedrooms. On different floors."

I lose the ability to access my cognitive functions for a moment. By the time I'm back online, F-man has located the pajama shirt I tossed into the corner of my bed-less bedroom on his way to what I can only assume is the next step of forced transportation—emptying my clothes into his bodyguards' arms so they all can dump me off in a th-

thirty-*thousand* square foot palace.

My current apartment is roughly five hundred square feet…so that means…the place F-man's talking about is roughly…sixty apartments.

Ha ha. I might scream.

F-man actually begins digging through my drawers, and that snaps me out of my coma. "What are—"

He waves a pair of holey underwear in my face. "What is this?"

"My *panties*!" I shriek. "What the—" I swear. "—are you *doing*?"

He rips sock after sock out, unrolls them, and stuffs his fingers in the holes. "Why does everything you own have holes? You're always so put together at work." He rips out a bra, examines the staining, the strap. He tugs on the elastic, or he tries to, at least. It's gone. It's been gone. No more elastic to speak of. "What the—" A breathless curse whispers from his gaping lips. His head begins shaking softly. "Marcella…" When he sees my face, something like sense snaps into him. He peers between me and the cheap, plain bra I've had since high school. Heat explodes in his cheeks, and he swears as he drops it back into my drawer. "I'm sorry." More swears. "I wasn't thinking. I'm so—" Swear. "—sorry."

Swallowing uninhibited rage, I mutter, "Are you done?"

"Y-yes."

"So you'll get out of my apartment now?"

"No." He swipes a hand down his face; it's trembling. "I'm dead serious, Marcella. I'm not leaving you here. And tomorrow, we're taking the day off to get you a new wardrobe."

"Do you even understand how much work it will be to adjust your schedule for that?"

"*Marcella*." Tone hard, he meets my eyes.

I flinch. "*Stop* saying my name. And *definitely* don't say it like *that*."

"You're my girlfriend, right?"

"I mean. Kinda?"

"How does your name on a legal document that says you're my girlfriend result in *kinda*?"

I cannot argue with the logic. Or, well, I *could*, but it would not make me correct, and then I'd feel gross. "Okay. You're absolutely right. Yes, I am your…girlfriend."

"An exemplary one, no less?"

I knew I'd regret saying that. Lips peeling back from my teeth, I fight my way through, "Y-eesss…?"

"Are you not also my assistant, who is under a different contract outlining that your availability is to be made around my schedule, outside of emergency situations involving health or familial disruptions?"

"Yes, I traded my soul to your company. That is a fact."

"So, as my assistant, arranging time for me to spend with my girlfriend whenever I deem is perfectly reasonable, and, as my girlfriend, letting me spoil you when I discover you lack basic needs is also perfectly reasonable, isn't it?"

I throw my hands in the air. "I don't know! Maybe in rich people land it's *reasonable* to give your girlfriend a *house* and buy her a new wardrobe on a whim, but I'm not *from* rich people land! The gunshot scared me. I appreciate you coming by and reminding me that a stray bullet most likely isn't going to come through my floor now that the cops are here. You have done your *perfectly normal boyfriend* duties. Must you be such an overachiever?"

"Yes, actually." His arms cross. "It's a compulsion of mine."

Oh my word.

His arms are crossed.

They're crossed.

Over his chest.

Because he's *upset*.

I've never seen this before.

The way the action displays his muscles is something I am entirely unprepared for.

"What are you looking at?" he asks.

My gaze drags up off his chest and to his face. I squeak, "Nothing."

Confusion knits his brows, but he lets it slide. "Marcella, please. If not for you, for your friend. Think of Penny. I can't imagine she'd want you to stay here if you had another option. I can't imagine that she's in a better situation if she can't give you a better option."

She...really isn't. She's a starving artist who takes that term too literally. She'll forget to eat almost daily because she's busy working two part-time minimum wage jobs and fighting in the weary evenings to get her projects off the ground before she passes out with a paintbrush in her hand.

If we were in the same building, I could work making sure she at least has dinner into my schedule. I could bring her water while she paints. It wouldn't be *so* bad. Probably less loud than my current neighbors.

Dropping my chin, I mutter, "That's playing dirty."

"I cannot find it in myself to care less."

My eyes close. "You suck." And, yet, for the first time in two months, I'm not certain I despise this side of him. "Fine. Let's hurry up and get going. I'll need to get a head start on phone calls and emails to adjust your schedule tomorrow morning. The soonest I can make it work is noon."

"Perfect. I'll take you to lunch. Think of where you'd like to go."

To bed. I would like to go to bed.

And, isn't it ironic, that in the four years since I was a

dorm student, I'm going to have a bed to go to…

The part where you mentioned wanting a functioning AC seventeen times in two hundred questions. Also, the police outside was a compelling factor in my lack of understanding.

– Finnegan

Chapter 7

I can't believe you followed through on getting me a Publix cake.

– Marcella

If I weren't aggressively shoving a Minecraft cake from Publix into my mouth right now, I don't think I'd be able to survive this experience. Sipping an iced coffee that magically appeared with the cake and F-man this morning, I furiously type what must be my fiftieth apology email concerning *Mr. Marsh's absence today* while seated at the marble island counter in what is *not* a mansion.

It's a freaking castle.

I could barely tell last night, as the moonlight fell upon the stone peaks and towers of the exterior, but it's a two-story castle. Complete with gardens and fountains, hot tubs and pools, twelve bathrooms, eight bedrooms, a movie theater, a separate garage. A glorious staircase leads up to double entry doors, for cryin' out loud.

Lavish is an understatement.

Luxurious does not begin to explain.

My beautiful, tall, curly-headed Penny drifts through the bright dining area before me, green eyes agleam. Her mouth hasn't shut since I had to buzz her in at the *gate*, which is roughly eight thousand miles away past luscious green lawns, sculptures, and topiaries.

"And…" she begins, prayerfully quiet, "…I can live here with Marciboo?"

Behind her, smile wide as ever, F-man says, "Yes."

"What if I break something?"

"I'll replace it."

"What's the rent?"

"No rent."

"What's the catch?"

"No catch."

My eyes roll. I mock mouth F-man as I pull a cupcake from the bottom layer of the Minecraft cake tower, pluck a paper cutout of the default avatar skin—dubbed Steve—off, and assemble a frosting sandwich.

Penny plants her hands at her hips and lifts her chin. "What if Marciboo doesn't marry you in November?"

"She already made me write up a contract that states I am not permitted to change the terms of your staying here for up to a year beyond November. There will be no rent and full coverage of amenities throughout the duration of your stay. If she doesn't marry me but continues to work for me beyond next November, the terms maintain until either of you want to leave." His eyes flick toward me. "That part isn't in the contract. But my dear *Marciboo* likes certainty, so let it be known. You are welcome here. For as long as you are content to stay."

Wistfully beautiful, Penny giggles and locks her hands behind her sweet little dress-clad back. "Marciboo does really like her contracts, doesn't she?"

Gaze still fixed and gentle on me, F-man murmurs, "It's a very adorable trait of hers."

My fingers inch toward the silverware drawer below the counter where I'm sitting. Eye twitching, I tell myself *not* to procure a butter knife and carve out my benevolent benefactor's jugular. If only for Penny's sake.

I grab another cupcake. Not a knife. A *cupcake*.

At the very least, this place *also* has an in-home gym, so even if exercise won't make up for a terrible diet, the opportunity to pretend it might diffuse some of the pure sugar soaring through my veins is available. I sure do love delusion.

"This seems a little too good to be true." Penny pinches her chin, scanning F-man up and down. Musical, she hums, then she shrugs, then she turns on her heel. "I've always wanted a dedicated space for an art studio. I'm going to see if I can't find a room with a nice garden view on the other side of the house." She stops short in her tracks a foot from the exit archway. "How attached are you to clean carpets? Specifically, if I find the perfect room, and it has carpet, and that carpet gets stained for some reason…with copious amounts of paint…"

"Replacing carpet isn't that expensive."

"Great! Love to hear it! Bye!" Penny's sunflower skirt dances as she skips out of view. I find myself shaking my head as I sign off another email with *Sincerely* instead of a more appropriate *End me*.

F-man settles onto the stool beside mine, and my fingers freeze over the keyboard halfway through the greeting of my next email.

He leans toward me, stops behind me, and reads over my shoulder. "You've written *I hope this email finds your corpse, as I desperately do not want to deal with your whiny reply, you copious little—*"

"I haven't edited it yet," I snip. "Have you never heard of *drafting*? There are two options with writing professional emails. The first, I stare at the screen for three hours, wondering what words are. The second, I *draft* in my own voice the necessary information, then I *edit* what

I've said into corporate tongue."

"Aren't you worried you'll accidentally press send too soon?"

"My send is set with a thirty second cancellation period. The only chance I don't undo it in time is if I click it by mistake then have a seizure. But, in that event, I think I'll have bigger problems to dwell on."

He makes a low, vibrating sound *way* too close to my ear. "Fascinating."

Scowling, I face F-man and freeze.

Barely three inches away, he rests his arm against the counter to support his prolonged *closeness* and searches my eyes. "Yes?"

Straightening my back, I say, "What do you think of Penny?"

"She's sweet. Your relationship with her baffles me… yet also gives me hope."

"So you like her?"

He murmurs, "I suppose."

"Want me to set you two up?"

His brows jump.

"You'd be *perfect* for each other. She loves shiny things, and smiling. I think she laughs a lot, too. She's basically a model. And the best part?"

"She won't daydream about stabbing me in my sleep?" he asks.

I point. "A pro to take into consideration, for sure, but no. *She* doesn't hate you. I'm pretty sure she'd love you for every reason that makes me find you unbearable." A little manic, I grin. "What do you say? I hook you up with a few cheat cards since I've known her for over a decade, I coordinate the wedding, and if you *ever* make her the smallest bit unhappy for even a moment, I promise to only wax off your eyebrows, not castrate you." I second-guess what I'm saying and furrow my brow. "Okay, well, actually, I'll only castrate you *a little bit*. That's the promise. Make her sad, never be a dad."

He rolls his lips into his mouth to subdue the laughter shaking his whole body. Battling to contain himself, he swipes his hand down his face and clears his throat. "Sorry. I'm not interested in Penny."

"Take that back right now."

"Why?"

"How can you *not* be interested in Penny? She's like a beautiful, voluptuous doll with that figure and those curls. She's innocent. She's darling. Many a male specimen falls to their knees upon seeing her. I'm offended you didn't bow when she got here. Have you no manners?" My eyes narrow. "Basically, there's not a single thing wrong with her, so what's wrong with you?"

Without clearance to do so, he lifts a finger and tucks my hair behind my ear. "You're absolutely right, pumpkin. There isn't a single thing wrong with your precious friend. I just can't picture her threatening to remove vital parts of my anatomy with very minimal prompting, and I expect at least that much from my women. Non-negotiable, really."

"Masochism," I mutter, shove my hair *off* my ear, and return my attention to my computer. "That's what's wrong with you. You're a masochist. This entire situation is so much clearer now. You didn't notice me until I filled out a form where you had me answer intimate questions that alluded to my true temperament and disgust. Now that I've told you I hate you, you're obsessed. Time for me to google *how to be nice to your boyfriend*. That'll end things real quick."

He laughs, over my shoulder, maintaining that *too closeness*. "Is it a breach of contract to try and set me up with your friend? I don't believe normal girlfriends would attempt such a thing."

He is probably correct. "I apologize for my behavior. How dreadfully un-real-girlfriend of me. I am out of practice. But, look—" I type *how to be nice to your boyfriend* into the search bar in a new tab. "—I'm actively attempting to remedy the situation." The page loads, and disgust riots in my gut.

"Ooh." His *breath* touches my neck. "Interesting." He puts his *chin* on my *shoulder.* "Go on. Step one. Remind me how much you adore me. Every day."

My breaths thin. My gaze glosses over with red. My fingers inch toward the silverware drawer again, but I stop myself just short of pulling it open and gouging out an eye. I know better than to do that. I am a mature adult. And I have a *system* in place for such a time as this. "*Pickles.*"

Exhaling a laugh, he kisses my cheek and stands. "Let me know when you're ready to go shopping, pumpkin. Also, I adore you. Not your understandably wonderful friend. You."

I stuff air into my lungs, scrub his nasty kiss off my face, and mutter, "You are not removing yourself from my presence fast enough. Detrimental bodily harm may occur in five, four, th—"

Lifting his hands in surrender, he escorts himself out of the kitchen, and I return to my emails.

Chapter 8

Give me a hint.

– Finnegan

"Studies show," my beautiful, stone-faced bride-to-be begins, "that single women are happier than single men. They also live longer than married women." Turning the bra she's looking at around, she glares at the tag, holds it up to her...um...yeah...and huffs before putting it back on the shelf. "I get that."

Being here feels incredibly illegal. An attendant just moments ago groped one of the other customers, who was only wearing lace. I did not know that happened in these sorts of frilly, pink and black, fine establishments...

Marcella, however, did because when we were greeted, the first words out of her mouth were: if you touch me, he's suing.

"Why is this over fifty dollars?" she mutters at a very pretty black bra with a lacy butterfly design for the back and a tiny bow in the front. Not that I am noticing anything other than a butterfly theme. No mention of butterflies made it into any of my form questions, but it's clear Marcella gravitates toward them.

Given her true personality, that she likes something so delicate is...cute.

"Cost is irrelevant," I remind her.

If looks could kill. It's like she's trying to incinerate me with her eyes. "I know you're not a pervert, Mr. Has Been Examining the Ceiling this Whole Time. So tell me why you decided we were going to start *here*."

"Because. You ate too many cupcakes for breakfast and didn't want to go out for lunch."

It takes everything in me not to laugh when her fists clench so hard and fast her knuckles crack. "You know what I mean. Why the underwear shopping *first*?"

I shouldn't play around like this if I actually want her to tolerate me by November, but the way she responds to everything I say is gold. "I figured this would be the most taxing part of shopping, so it would be best to tackle it while you have all your stamina."

She relaxes, turning back to the row of neatly folded and displayed undergarments. "Valid thought process. Sometimes I forget you're intelligent."

"That was almost a compliment."

"It was a compliment."

I laugh. "You're not very good at compliments."

She picks up something pink. "I am, actually, extremely good at compliments. I have a knack for paying attention to details, and the more detailed a positive observation, the more it means to someone. For example, your shirt today brings out the blue in your eyes and complements your hair well. An excellent choice."

I glance down at the green shirt I'm wearing. It is the very one she put with this pair of pants and arranged in my closet alongside the rest of my outfits for this week—which include both my business attire and my after-work clothes. "Are you complimenting yourself?

Her lips quirk up into a smirk. "Absolutely. And I've done an amazing job."

I bite my lip and cross one arm over my chest to grip my bicep. Tapping my fingers against the muscle, I watch Marcella continue her perusal.

No one should be this funny.

No one should always have a well-thought-out comeback at the ready like she does.

There has to be a limit to how clever someone is allowed to be.

"My underwear has never matched before..." She holds up a full, scandalous, set of pink lingerie, complete with both top and bottom pieces. "If I get in a car wreck, the paramedics are going to be *so* proud of me."

It becomes mildly difficult to swallow, and my heart jumps as she tosses the entire set over her arm.

Casually coming in here was a less-than-fantastic idea, I think. Picturing Marcella in a full set of pink does unhelpful things to my brain. I don't believe I have ever been invested enough in a woman to let my thoughts wander where they are right now.

Pink makes her seem so much more gentle than she is.

It's devastating to my emotional health, but I can't stop myself from wondering what would suit her the best...

My evil gaze drifts across mannequins and displays, taking in styles and shades. It's a proper women's undergarment store, not a risque one, but that doesn't mean I should allow my head to picture Marcella modeling pin-up style in everything my attention grazes.

Unfortunately, the sewer that is my mind works religiously through creating the feature photos for scandalous calendars until its working on a spring two years away.

When Marcella takes herself to the back, I automatically trail after, stopping the second her destination becomes clear.

The dressing rooms.

"You're welcome to go in with her," an attendant, whose shirt is gaping to display *product in use*, informs me.

Expression sour, Marcella makes direct eye contact with the poor woman, snips, "*Incorrect*," and slams the door shut.

"Oh." The woman laughs. "Don't tell me." She lowers her voice. "You're in trouble? Just so you know, underwear isn't a good apology gift."

I smile. "It's not an apology gift. This is how she always is."

The woman's brows knit. "O-oh?"

"This is uncomfortable, and I'm dying," Marcella abruptly calls past the door, causing the attendant to jump.

Shrugging in what I hope is a mildly sympathetic manner, I call back, "Which one?"

"Pink set. My disappointment is immeasurable. What will the paramedics think now?"

Not what I'm thinking right now. Which is great.

She swears. "I know, I know, baby."

My face heats. Before I realize she's talking to a bra.

"Unfortunately, breathing *is* mandatory. Shh. *Shh*, please don't cry. I still love you. We just can't be together."

Scarlet, I find myself biting my lip again to stifle yet another onslaught of laughter.

When the dressing room door whirls open, I still haven't completely recovered my composure, so Marcella shoots me a disgusted look before turning to the attendant and losing all her ire in a single blink. "Your store is very tidy and well organized. I apologize for my personality. I mean no disrespect." With another blink, she's trying to kill me with her eyes again. "I want this one. Let's go."

My eyes fix on the black butterfly bra. "Don't you need more than one?"

"No."

"Don't you need..." I don't want to say *panties*. I already should be locked up for coming in here, but, well, Marcella refused to accept my card when I tried to hand it to her in the limo.

Her eyes said *suffer*, and I leaned into my fate.

"You can get a six pack for ten bucks at Walmart. Those are the kind I'm familiar with. Since my effort to branch out resulted in pain, I would like to go to Walmart now and get the exact same things I have always gotten. Plus this." She splays the butterfly side of the bra, looking at it almost tenderly. "This sparks joy. I will condemn myself to the pain for her."

Mm. Yeah.

I think it's unavoidable.

I may very swiftly be falling in love with this woman.

"If that's all you want, I feel the need to reiterate how poor a job you're doing of being a gold digger."

"Untrue." She trots her cute pant-suited self up to the register. Once she's handed the bra to the woman behind it, she braces an elbow against the counter and looks at me. "I already have plans to abuse your funds at Walmart. Don't worry."

I'm really not worried. At all.

"That loaf of bread was only a dollar at full price," I say, as Marcella opens the plain white french loaf in the back of the limo.

"Your point?" She lays the forty-seven cent bread beside her, atop a pathetic number of plastic bags.

"Why did you get it off the clearance cart?"

Sitting across from me, she tears open a bag of Sargento cheddar cheese sticks. "Because these were *five* dollars." She peels one out of its plastic prison and tears the heel off her bread, seeming subtly pleased with herself when she says, "A week more of this and you'll be broke."

She bites into them together.

I find myself inexplicably entranced and mulling over all the times in these past two months that I've sat across from her, bored out of my mind, as she smiled calmly while working away on her tablet. She was hiding so much spice beneath her composed façade.

Snapping out of the spell, I say, "Please tell me you don't think that's a meal. I was hoping to take you to dinner once you ran out of cupcake energy."

She licks her lips. "I got hungry. Dinner wasn't available. Walmart discount bread cart and cheese were." She settles in. "Man, I love bread cart."

"I take it you don't cook much?" I murmur.

Mouth full, she blinks at me and swallows. "What an offensive question. Can't you tell this recipe has been passed down in my family for generations?" Realization crosses her expression, and she removes another stick from the bag before passing me both it and a new torn piece of bread. "Girlfriend behavior. Couples share food. I excel at this."

She is...such a strange creature.

I'd very much like to put her in my pocket and take her with me everywhere.

Assembling the cheese bread, I turn my attention out the window, at the buildings easing by.

This is nice.

Not the cheese bread.

It might be the cheapest thing I've had in my entire life. But...

Okay, maybe it's not so bad.

"Hey."

I pull myself from my thoughts and find Marcella opening another cheese stick. "Yes?" I ask.

She nudges her chin at the rest of my bread chunk and cheese. "What do you think?"

"I think if you're trying to make our first date a disaster so I won't want another one, you are doing a very poor job of it."

She goes still. "Are you serious?"

"Quite." Smiling, I relax and tear off a surprisingly light and buttery piece of bread. "I've had a most splendid time thus far, and I am eager to continue."

"Continue? There's more?"

"You've not gotten any new outfits."

"I got unmentionables, socks, and pajamas at Walmart. My suits are nice. I don't need day clothes."

I hum. "Are you sure about that? There's a difference between attending events with me as my assistant and as my date. You need evening gowns for balls, fine dining. Casual attire for yacht parties, movie premiers. It may even be prudent to get you athletic wear. Once the seasons change, I'd like to take you apple picking, pumpkin carving, to a haunted house, on a hayride...all sorts of things that aren't easy to do in a suit."

"Bonfire?"

"Excuse me?"

"When it gets colder, I always want to burn things, but my family has never had the space, so I resort to lining up a dozen tea candles and huddling near them for warmth while I bask in the flickering glow. You have a large yard. At *both* your local homes. We could set things on fire."

I beam. "My girlfriend's an arsonist."

Wary, she surveys me. "I don't want to know why that excites you." Heaving a breath, she finishes her food, twists the tie back onto the bread bag, and folds her arms. "What happened to you while you were growing up that left you with a twisted desire for abuse?"

Whoa, left turn.

My mind flips through memories of my childhood, private schools, tutors, busy parents, jealous friends, toys to fill the gaps between emotional connections. My mother was always in the kitchen. Baking, cooking, sending me off with elaborate snacks that the kids would tease me about. She insisted we all sit down for meals together, as a family, whenever possible. I lost my father earlier than most, but Marcella knows that. The news covered it and plastered my grief everywhere while I stepped up to fill his shoes. She doesn't know about Mom's declining mental state because I've managed to keep it out of the public eye.

Even before the dementia started setting in, Mom preferred to stay out of Dad's spotlight. She was the silent strength that held us together and gave us something normal while I was groomed to be heir and Dad's new businesses kept taking off, just like my grandfather's had.

She was everything to us.

She is still everything to me.

Even on the days when I'm not certain she remembers exactly who I am.

"Are you...okay?" Marcella asks after I fear I've been quiet too long. I refocus to find her looking overly concerned about someone she claims to hate. Unease apparent, she says, "You stopped smiling. Was your childhood really that bad?"

My head shakes. "No. It was great."

Her fingers dig past her suit jacket as she grips her arm. "Are you thinking about your father?"

A sting pierces my chest. It's been years. I wish I were used to life without him by now. I'm just...not. "I miss him. He was a good...a good dad."

"I'm sorry."

I force a small smile before putting energy into finishing my bread and cheese. "To answer your first question, I don't think I have a twisted desire for abuse. I suppose I simply don't find you particularly abusive."

"Assuming you aren't a masochist, what is it that has you interested in me when I'm not a very enjoyable person to be around?"

"Who told you that?"

"Literally everyone but my parents and my two friends." Her head tilts. "Scratch that. Literally everyone but my two friends. My parents tried to fix me, like good parents do in an effort to create suitable members of society, but eventually they realized I was a lost cause. The blunt meanness was in my veins." A cynical smile twists her lips. "Get this, periodically throughout my kid years, Mom would do little at-home tests to check that I wasn't a sociopath. I'll never forget the conversation we had about all of it once I was older. I guess she thought I struggled with empathy."

"Do you?"

A funny look weasels its way into her eyes as she fixes her attention outside. "I don't think so. I feel *so much* when I choose to. I *have* empathy. It's just that, most of the time, I don't really care. Why should I? If I tried to care about everything all the time, I'd destroy myself. It's better to care a whole lot about the few people who have proven themselves worthy of that energy." Relaxing, she shrugs. "I don't know. That's what I think, anyway. Who knows… maybe I am a sociopath, and I'm just fooling myself because I have a good enough grasp on the logical progression behind emotional expression to respond correctly and I do occasionally go out of my way to do so."

My heart constricts, dully thudding in my ears. This

woman... My lips part. "What makes someone worthy of your care?"

She scoffs. "Wouldn't you like to know?"

"Yes. I really would."

Her eyes roll; the action reflects in the sunlit window. "Well, I can't tell you. Part of being enough for me is being enough for yourself, which means you aren't allowed to teach yourself how to be someone else."

I arch a brow. "*Unless*...a paycheck's involved."

She sniffs. "That is the notable exception, yes. I've deduced that it is likely hard to be yourself when you're starving in a cardboard box off main street."

The incessant pound of my heart in my head grows stronger with every moment. "If it would help, I think I could change at least a little. For you."

She doesn't even bother looking at me. "That is not how anything works. People don't change; they grow. Sadly, that means you're only going to get happier and more energetic." Her voice takes on tragic airs. "I pity my future, should my employment last."

Strange. I pity my future should it not.

Before her, my assistant was an amicable young man who couldn't maintain the demand of working for me when his wife got pregnant. Before him, it was a woman who saw her chance to take advantage of me at the height of my grief after my father passed.

Once I'd managed to turn that woman down with a smile, I threw furniture.

I can hardly remember a time I've been so mad. So... disappointed. So hurt.

Even if Marcella hasn't been acting like herself for the past two months, her professional consistency has always been comforting and reliable. Now that she's transparent, I don't think I've ever met anyone half so secure.

I've come to value her presence and the peace her capable airs bring.

Being around her has let me be myself without worrying how she'd respond.

Being around her, from the first day, has been safe.

No.

– Marcella

Chapter 9

I should have pushed you down the stairs.

– Marcella

He's...*lingering*.

There are approximately seventeen million bags of extravagant clothes in the castle room I have claimed as my own. They drown out my little lump of Walmart bag familiarity quite considerably, and I am not looking forward to sorting through them. I'm already drowning in a puddle of foreign luxuries.

The only reason I'm not sobbing and puking is because —sweet baby of air condition—there are *vents*. In the *ceilings*. And *multiple* thermostats. Including one in the room I picked.

It is literally the only reason I picked the room I did last night. I stomped right through this extravagant mansion, stopped at the first room I found with a thermostat in it, and dumped my stuff on the bed before curling up on the couch that also happened to be in the room I picked.

Holding back laughter, F-man pulled a soft throw down over me, ignored when I hissed at him, and told me to sleep well.

Crossing my arms, I lean against the locked side of the front double doors and arch a brow. "What is happening right now?"

F-man smiles—but of course he does. He hasn't stopped smiling since he convinced me that it was absolutely girlfriend behavior to show him every outfit I tried on, as long as it fit and I didn't hate it with every ounce of blood in my body. "What do you mean?" he asks.

"I said *goodbye*. Go back to your little limo and your little bodyguards. This is my house now. This was a first date. I don't partake of intimacies without more commitment, so if you're waiting around for a goodnight kiss, I'm going to slam the door in your face and tell my dear sweet Penny that you've assaulted me. Nothing burns worse than her scathing disapproval. Her lips pinch, and she does this thing." I try to imperceptibly shake my head a mere half inch either direction, then I groan and sag. "I can't do it right, but, trust me, it destroys self-esteem."

"I'm not waiting for a kiss."

"Oh. Excellent." I delay a moment. "Am I unaware of some other ritual that would breach my contract of *act like a girlfriend*?"

He braces his arm against the door, leaning in too close while his free hand dances taps against his thigh. "I can't help but notice…you haven't said my name this entire day."

Dread hits the pool of derision in my gut. "Guess it hasn't come up."

"Why don't you try a *goodnight, Finn* on for size?"

A swallow sticks in my throat. "No, I don't think I will."

"Are you still calling me *Mr. Marsh* in your head? Or perhaps you've never thought of me as Mr. Marsh. I'll accept whatever insulting moniker you've blessed me with as a nickname."

I will throw myself down the front steps and die before

I tell him I've been calling him *F-man* in my head for the past day. "Sorry. In full recognition of the fact my hatred is largely uncalled for, I have maintained mental respect for you as my boss. You have not warranted any clever code names amongst my friends. And, truly, I do my best not to think about you at all."

He rests his head against his arm. "That makes me sad. It's like you're saying I've been of such little consequence, I'm not worth a speck of energy beyond what you are obligated to provide."

I suck my teeth and avert my eyes.

"Ow."

"What can I say? I'm a big fan of separating the professional and the personal…"

"You don't have the kind of job that allows such a thing. I have called you at two in the morning and told you we're flying to Japan in an hour."

I stretch my lips into a smile. "I know, and I still haven't forgiven you."

"I bought you a lunch shaped like a cat to apologize for the inconvenience."

"It took every last bit of my acting skills to gracefully behead that cat without letting on that the ketchup placement was fully intentional."

Bathed in dusky shadows, he chuckles. His hand— edged in moonlight—lifts, and I tense as it draws near. "Sorry," he murmurs, inches from my face. "May I cup your cheek?"

"I don't foresee enjoying that."

His fingers close, but his hand doesn't lower. "You aren't actually all that affectionate, are you?"

"I'm really not. I have been known to hit children who touch me unexpectedly." I grimace, too aware that his hand is still hovering. "Listen. We're *really* different people. I

84

can't be whatever it is you're looking for even if my answers to your form questions amused or impressed you. On paper, we're both smart enough to seem complementary, but I'm not going to be whatever you need to fill whatever you're trying to inside. If you need comfort to feel loved, if you need expressions of touch or romantic words, that's not how I operate."

"How do you operate when you love someone? How do your friends know you love them?"

Static buzzes in my head. My gaze drifts off his face. I search the pristine stone porch at his feet. "I don't... I don't know. Brigid was the only person in my high school who didn't annoy me. I approached her and asked if she had a vacancy for a friend. Later, Brigid found Penny, and I thought she was insane, because Penny has *always* been this bubbly monstrosity, but—" Swearing, I laugh. "—no. Brigid was right. Penny gets us."

"Has it just been the three of you since?"

"Yeah. No one else liked us much. Well, okay. Boys liked Penny, but no one else liked us, and we didn't like them, so we didn't let them touch her."

"Interesting..." His attention slips over my every inch. "And you don't know how you love them even though you clearly adore them with everything in you?"

Eyes rolling skyward, I free an irritated sigh. "I've never thought about it before. I guess...*maybe*...when I love someone, I try to fulfill their needs. Whatever that may be in the moment. I just want them to be happy, so I try to become the pieces they're missing from their happiness."

"That's beautiful, Marcella."

"Shut up. What are you even still doing here?"

His head shakes. "I'm waiting for my *goodnight, Finn*."

My lip curls. "Are you sure you sent your order to the right location?"

He settles himself in a little deeper, as though preparing to stay here all night. "Pretty positive. Why don't you like my name?"

"I don't dislike your name. Do I think it's stupid? Sure. A little bit. It has too many letters."

"Our names have the same number of letters."

"Too many syllables then," I mutter.

He tilts his face a fraction closer, whispering, "I have some bad news, Mar-cel-la."

"Ugh!" I snap. "It's just too intimate to call you by your first name, okay? It changes everything about how I compartmentalize our relationship in my head, and haven't I had enough change for one week?"

His nod...it's almost amicable...almost understanding. Unfortunately, he then opens his mouth. "So what you're saying is you would address your boyfriend by his last name or not at all? If so, I'll accept it. However, if not, I think your aversion *might* be a breach of contract."

"*This* is why I wanted the terms of our contract laid out more clearly, so you couldn't pull this kind of *crap*."

"Marcella. I'm not pulling anything. If you tell me this is how you'd treat your boyfriend, I'll accept it and rescind my earlier request that you use my name or endearments. It was wrong of me to assume how you'd naturally act with your significant other in any respect."

I have been on precious few romantic excursions—all of them disappointing—but never once did I call any of those chuckleheads by their last name with an honorific. "Once upon a time," I mutter, "I graduated high school, and I had the devastating experience of meeting a teacher in a store the following summer. When I greeted her, I used *Mrs. Blackwood*. She said I could call her *Helen* now that I'd graduated. This is the first time I've ever said her name. It is also the last." I lift my arm between us. "*Look.*

Goosebumps. I've broken a law of the universe."

His hand moves, skimming across my raised hair, and I jerk. "Do *not*."

Wincing, he pockets his hand. "Sorry. I understand. Change isn't just painful for you. It's uncomfortable and disturbing. May I present my point of view?"

"If you must."

"Mrs. Blackwood is the title you used when Helen was your teacher. It's how you associate her in your head as your teacher. Associating her with *Helen* removes the weight of her role. You aren't willing to let that go because to you it's not correct to change that history or alter your relationship now. Just because you graduated doesn't mean she earned the closeness you associate with removing her title." He wets his lips. "I am very serious about marrying you, Marcella. I understand your reservations and your concerns where our characters appear to collide; however, in your eyes, have I not paid a lot of money for a chance? In your eyes, is it right for you to intentionally distance us? To intentionally keep me in the *purely business* compartment of your brain, if that is what you're subconsciously doing? Have I not earned the right to ask that you change how you consider our relationship?"

I hate him. I really hate him. But, again, he isn't *wrong*. He has paid a lot of money for a chance to escape the business box in my skull. There's just one important thing he's entirely neglecting. "Mr. Marsh, you hold all the power in both our relationships. If you change your mind about me after I spend any time reprogramming mine where you're concerned, I'll be stuck with the emotional weight of undoing it all."

"You're afraid you'll come to like me and I'll lose interest?"

I don't meet his eyes. "I'm too good at pretending. I

don't trust you enough to take the chance I'll trick myself into finding you less annoying than I do just because you're nice to me. If we're treating this like a trial run relationship, I require the grace to keep my distance until I trust that you're safe. In different ways, that's how new relationships start—with caution, boundaries, and walls. You've paid for the chance to have conversations like these after spending a lot of off-the-clock time together, but money can't earn you any rights where my emotions are concerned."

"That is more than reasonable."

I drag my attention up, wait for a *but*. It doesn't come.

Instead, he says, "Is there anything I can do within the constraints of this trial that would help level the power discrepancy between us?"

"Short of making me a joint owner of your bank accounts and businesses, I think I'm kind of stuck. I'll have to deal with being in a position where I have no actual legal or personal rights outside your moral code. The discrepancy comes down to money in the end. I can't afford to protect myself. Thankfully, I don't think you're a bad person, but what do I really know about you? The biggest thing you have going for you so far is that very few people allow me this kind of consideration to explain myself without getting defensive. I appreciate when people are mature enough to talk to me until we can understand each other." Clearing my throat, I lift my hand and awkwardly provide my…boyfriend…with a shoulder pat of appreciation. "Anyway. Good talk. Goodnight."

I'm turning around when he says, "Okay."

Something in his tone strikes me as odd, so I peer back at him.

Much too pensive and lenient, he bites his bottom lip and hums. "Setting you up with joint access and permissions now rather than later makes little difference to me. I'd provide nothing less for my wife. If having access to the ability to abuse my funds early on in our relationship makes you more comfortable, it is simple enough."

My mouth drops open. "Are you insane?"

"I don't think so. Can you put situating this into my schedule?"

I blurt, "*No*. I don't want to be on your accounts! We've only known each other for two months and change."

"You are sending me extremely mixed messages, pumpkin."

Stomping, I jab him in the chest with my finger. "I am not. *You* asked a question. I gave you the *correct* answer. Emotions were not involved previously because the correct answer is insane and something you shouldn't even joke about considering. I could be a con-woman for all you know."

Far too *chill*, he smiles down at my finger on his chest. "A con-woman. Playing the long game."

"Not even. *Long game* would be dating and marrying you, then siphoning away your funds into a private account for ten years before either divorcing you or vanishing. It would be wearing too much makeup and batting my eyelashes to distract you when you mention prenups. It would be throwing a tantrum and saying you don't love me if you insist. Two months is *not* a long game."

"Should I be concerned at how much thought you've given this?"

I open my mouth to tell him I came up with everything I just rambled on the spot, but seeing as that doesn't help my case, I snip, "Yes," instead.

His smile tips a little too close to *cocky* for my liking. "You have given this absolutely zero thought, haven't you?"

Removing my finger from his chest, I widen my stance

and plant my hands at my hips. "My resentment of you grows with every passing moment."

"I expect this task to be on my schedule within the week. As your boss, that's an order."

My spine straightens so sharply it curves backwards, a la reverse shrimp. "Oh. Oh, I see. You give your employees *orders* now? Do excuse my impertinence, m'lord."

"*M'lord,*" he murmurs, eyes glittering in the moonlight. "That's an interesting nickname to give me. It feels mildly suggestive, though. Are you comfortable with that?"

"I will put leeches in your pillowcase the next time I set up your clothes. Don't test me."

He splays his fingers.

I stare at them. "What is that?"

"Give me your left hand."

"No."

"Please?"

"Will you go away if I do?"

"Reluctantly, yes."

Groaning deeply, I let my head roll back as I place my hand in his.

The annoying sound of a jewelry case opening resonates in his pocket before he slips a stunning rose gold ring on my finger. The metal curls and twists, tiny leaf vines encircling a round-cut pale orange gem. At first glance, it's beautiful. At second...it's a pumpkin.

His grip solidifies when I attempt to rip my hand out of his.

"Let me go, you—"

"I'm not asking you to marry me. I already have. But start wearing this when you begin seriously considering saying *yes*." He drops a kiss to my knuckles. "Parting is such sweet sorrow."

My flesh absolutely crawls against the softness of his

lips brushing me. "Yea, that the dread of seeing you hence may consume my blissful solitude."

Freeing me with a laugh, he steps back. "I don't want to go home."

"I hadn't noticed."

"It's cold there." He takes another step back, toward the stairs.

Half my attention fixates on the edge he's blindly approaching. "Yes, a functioning air conditioning tends to do that to a place. I'm not amused by your bragging rights."

Another step. "Without the contempt of your heated gaze, what could hope to keep me warm?"

"A bonfire."

He slips.

I lunge forward just in time for his foot to plant on the stable platform of the next stair. In a cruel twist of fate, he catches me, leaving me staring speechless into his eyes.

Wordlessly, he ascertains that I'm stable on my feet, then he turns like he didn't just do anything on purpose.

I watch him descend the rest of the steps, get into the backseat of his limo, and drive off the property. When he's no longer in sight, I take myself to my room, adjust the thermostat so it's *freezing*, and begin sorting through the bags on my floor.

Chapter 10

It's not exactly a moat…but I'll accept drowning here.

– Marcella

"I must admit," Brigid, sprawled atop a plastic pink float in the massive pool outside my and Penny's castle mansion, murmurs, "it is difficult to argue with the benefits."

"Try harder," I mutter.

Paddling adorably in her floral swim cap, Penny does her laps around the deep end, AKA the only part of the entire pool where she can't touch the bottom. "He's told you he doesn't even need the *husband and wife* stuff. Can we abandon all our morals and just go through with it, for the *perks*?"

Seated on the shallow end steps, head just above the water, I glare at my friends. Who suck, by the way. "Clearly, you can."

"While I was growing up, my sister said she was going to sell me to the prince of a foreign country for oil shares. This is totally a better deal than that." Penny beams, catching all the sunlight.

"Marsh only wants company," Brigid says, lamely kicking her way over to the side where a tray of treats and drinks rest in the shade. Without any prompting at all, the housemaid Teresa set us up a little buffet, smiled, and went back inside to make sure I would never see dust again. Plucking a strawberry, Brigid takes a bite. "If you're adamantly against this, let me ask Cody if he's okay with letting me be a billionaire's special friend."

"I don't think Cody's the type to share."

"Never mind asking, then. He's a firefighter. Long shifts. What he doesn't know won't hurt him."

Oh. Okay. I get it. Screw morals. We no longer have consciences, period.

Must've missed that memo.

Leaning back, I let my legs float while I hold onto the metal railing that cuts down the center of the steps. "Nobody cares about my emotions anymore. Not now that they have access to a *pool*."

"A pool in Georgia is a very important thing." Brigid lifts one of the martini glasses, sniffs the contents, and takes a sip. "Hey, Pens. I don't think this is alcoholic. It seems to be frozen lemonade."

Gasping, Penny flippers her way over. "Yay! Juice."

Non-alcoholic martinis…

Probably because F-man's worried what other billionaire wife positions I'll apply for if I get drunk again. Jokes on him. I now have PTSD whenever I so much as look at a form.

"I've been keeping a horrible secret from you both," I begin, pitifully.

My friends, sipping their martinis, glance my way.

As dramatic as humanly possible, I face the pool wall. "When he stole me away from my beloved home and dumped me off here…he told me to bring *only* the *necessities*."

"That makes logical sense. He also then immediately bought you everything you would ever need, so letting you take anything with you from that molded-over apartment

93

was merciful. He could have wrapped you up in a towel like a stressed dog and wrangled you into the back of his limo." Brigid does not sound sympathetic to my immense struggles at all.

But I have barely scratched the surface.

"You don't understand. He insulted the penguin pebbles."

"*No!*" Penny's gasp rings in my ears like the validation I so desperately require.

I let my lip jut. "It's true. He said, and I quote, 'Why do you need that bucket of rocks?'"

While I was curled up in my throw blanket. Like a traumatized creature. Hugging my bucket of rocks and ambling to my car.

I will not specify that his tone was wholly curious and entirely friendly.

Because when isn't it?

Brigid in all her good sense drawls, "Why *did* you need the bucket of penguin pebbles? There were literal cops outside. Your awful neighbors were firing *guns*. Your penguin friends would have graciously understood leaving their pebbles behind until the next day."

I scowl at Brigid. "You have lost your way."

Pushing her wet, straight black hair over her shoulder, she says, "At least I don't get drunk and fill out marriage candidate tests."

"Yeah. Because you don't have to. Because *someone* already introduced you to your husband." It was me. I did it. "If only I'd had that same courtesy provided me. By my *so-called* penguin friends."

Penny, halfway through a second martini, which I think was supposed to be mine, says, "Girls, girls. Please don't quarrel. Remember, one of us has neither husband nor billionaire boyfriend who wants to give her his credit card."

94

Brigid pats Penny's swim cap. "Perspective. You're right. At least we aren't sad like you. Have a strawberry."

While Penny nibbles on the offered strawberry, I sag underwater and blow bubbles until I am completely out of air. Without full lungs, I've sunk against the bumps of the stairs. And before my heart starts to starve, I convince myself I could live on the pool floor forever. There's a peace in the sensory deprivation of it.

Once my organs are crying and rioting against their evil dictator, I plunge into the air and push water off my face.

"Oh good," Brigid says. "I thought we were about to witness a second suicide in your family."

"First attempts rarely bear fruit." I fold my arms. "Bold of you to assume the odds aren't stacked against me."

Endearingly gentle, Penny smiles. "We came up with a brilliant plan while you were contemplating mortality."

I arch a brow.

"It's simple, really." Brigid plucks a cube of sweating cheese off the treat platter and brings it to her lips. "Accept it if you dare."

I'm daring sometimes. On the weekends, usually.

And, wouldn't you know, it's the first Sunday of September...

"Okay. Hit me. What devious plot have you two concocted?"

The grins they throw each other do not inspire much confidence at all.

Chapter 11

Not to be dramatic, but **pickaxes your crops.**

– Marcella

Let the records show, I am against this.

Completely and utterly against this.

"I swear to—" I curse. "—if you try to give me that bouquet one more time, Marshipan…" Furiously, I decline *Marshipan's* gift on *Stardew Valley*. The *gall* of him to desecrate this sacred space by acting like *this*. I can't believe I took my stupid friends' stupid advice last Sunday to let him play with us—purely for research purposes. In a matter of hours, he's wriggled his way into my friend group like an evil worm. If I saw him on the sidewalk on a sunny day, *I'd step on him*. "And *you*—" I hiss at my giggling mansion-mate, who is seated on the couch across from me in the massive central living room. "—if you tell him *anything* else, I'm rage quitting this farm. If he wants to play *Stardew Valley* with us, it's his duty to read the Wiki like a proper noob."

"Eventually, your finger will slip and you'll click *yes*." F-man's low voice hums through my headphones, taunting and wicked.

"Technically," Brigid begins in a tone that puts me on edge, "accepting the bouquet means you're girlfriend and boyfriend. Aren't you under contract to be girlfriend and boyfriend, Marci?"

Wow.

Wowww.

I'm going to kill one of my best friends. I am going to slash my friend count in half.

She's *so* lucky she's not the friend living with me.

If she were, this mansion would stage a murder mystery in *hours*.

Monotone, I say, "You're dead to me."

On screen, F-man's little character comes hopping toward mine while I'm organizing my inventory at our community chest collection. When the bouquet appears in his hands again, I close out of the inventory window and bolt. "*Get away from me!*"

"Bridge has a point!" he defends.

"*No, she doesn't.* Stardew is *not* real life! You haven't even experienced my *two* heart event! To give me that thing, you need to reach my eight heart event!"

He chases me around the main farm house, which belongs to Brigid since this is her save.

On the porch, she drinks a coffee.

Penny loses it, giggling herself into a puddle on the floor in front of the couch in real life. Twisting around, she places her laptop on the cushions and wiggles merrily. "You have it tough, Marshipan. Every farm we've ever played together, Marciboo rooms with Krobus. She skips marriage altogether in favor of the sewer blob roommate."

"Slander," I hiss as I realize something truly horrible.

I...am smiling.

"Sewer blob?" F-man asks.

"We aren't there yet," Brigid informs. "He's a friendly monster who sells things in the sewers. You can invite him to be your roommate when you build enough of a

97

relationship with him."

"Fascinating," F-man murmurs.

I am never telling these back-stabbing ingrates that I've downloaded mods that turn Krobus into a dark elf and add heart events to his story. So what if the strange, outcast monster in the sewers is my favorite character? I feel a close personal connection to him.

Sue me.

"I've looked him up," F-man notes, despondently. "Pumpkin, these beauty standards are unattainable."

"Screw you, Marshi."

"Well…if you're offering…"

Penny squeaks, covering her ears and falling against the carpet. "My innocence!"

Her face is actually turning red over there on the other side of the room.

Bless.

"Ma'am?" Teresa scares the living daylights out of me from behind.

Yanking my headphones down around my neck, I face her. "Teresa. Hi! What's up?" She has a plate of food. Two, actually. That's peculiar.

Smiling, she offers me one. "Mr. Marsh messaged thirty minutes ago and told me to prepare dinner for you."

"Oh." Taken aback, I reach for the plate of steaming green beans and fish fillets. "This looks amazing, thank you."

Nodding, she makes her way to the other side of the room where Penny is.

What a role reversal if F-man's making sure *I* eat. That's quite literally in my job description. Also, what time is it if this is *dinner*?

Once I find my phone and the clock, I learn that the four of us have been playing *Stardew Valley* for seven hours straight, burning away our Saturday since right after a late lunch.

When I put my headphones back on, Brigid is saying, "I better make sure my hubby has something to eat when he gets home. Can we quit after this night?"

My mouth opens to offer some helpful advice on how her husband should learn to fend for himself—even though I know full well he works twelve-on, twelve-off shifts—but F-man beats me to the punch. "Sure. Pumpkin, do you mind staying on the call after your friends pull out? There's something I wanted to talk to you about."

Dread. Immediate, nausea-inducing dread. "I do mind, but I will oblige."

"I appreciate it."

Once we all tuck into our game beds, our farm saves, so I wave goodnight to Penny, grab my laptop and dinner, then head to my room with just F-man left on the line. When silence pervades, I take a shot at breaking it. "Marshi? Are you still there?"

"Sorry, yes. Is it just us? I'm new to Discord, so I wasn't sure if your friends were still listening in."

The fact he wants this to be super private gives me copious amounts of anxiety.

I double check the call. "It's just us. What's up? Is this work-related or…the other stuff?"

"Both."

Ugh. Great.

He plows on without giving me a moment to regret my life choices. "It's been two weeks since our last date, yet you're still not on my accounts. It's unusual for you to drop the ball on something important like this. I wanted to check in and make sure everything is okay. How's the family? Is there anything going on that's distracting you from your work?"

I nearly choke on a bite of fillet. "I *know* you aren't talking to me like that."

Humor in his tone, he says, "I'm very concerned. If there's anything I can help you with, please let me know."

Plopping onto the *massive* fluffy bed, which I have refused to sleep in out of spite, I set my laptop beside me and prop my dinner on my lap. "Do you think you're being funny?"

"Absolutely."

"Am I laughing?"

"I cannot be blamed for your lousy sense of humor."

Unamused, I nibble a green bean. "That may be the meanest thing you've ever said to me."

He laughs softly. "Sorry. I—"

"Do it again."

The longer it takes for him to respond, the more joy I find myself feeling.

Coughing, he manages a muffled, "Pumpkin, remember how you asked me something about having a twisted desire for abuse?"

"Maybe I do. Maybe I don't. The real question is: are you pressing your fist to your mouth and turning tomato red?"

"Perhaps," he murmurs.

"Lame."

"My heart was unprepared for you to flirt with me."

I nibble another green bean. "Playing Stardew always puts me in an uncharacteristically good mood. Also, you achieved a nickname against my best intentions. Don't get caught off guard. I am livid. For many reasons. Primarily, I don't want to hear anything more about joining your accounts. And I don't want to hear you insult my work ethic, unless you commit to the bit and do it properly."

He hums. "Mind describing what 'doing it properly'

100

looks like?"

My mind whirls into places it shouldn't while my fork hovers an inch from my lips. "No. I don't think I will."

His sigh pours into my skull, surround sound. Moments pass, then a vaguely disappointed noise follows. "I just looked up *how do I bully my girlfriend*, and I have been given a help line."

"Yeah, the algorithm sucks. Always trying to get people to go to therapy for some reason. It's a real scam." For the second time in the same exact hour, I discover that I am smiling. "I'd tell you what to actually look up in order to get the results you need, but I don't think you can handle the language."

He exhales a laugh. "You are sincerely baffling, Marcella. May I take you out tomorrow, on a date?"

My smile slips away. "I mean, I was planning to stare at the ceiling for prolonged lengths of time and refuse to get up until my bladder filed a formal complaint, but…"

"I guess you're still sleeping on the couch, huh?"

I bristle. "What gives you that idea?"

"The bed in the room you chose has a canopy. No ceiling to stare at without getting up. And you, my dear, take things too literally to have ignored that detail."

My gaze slips skyward, toward the thick fabric of the canopy. Choosing to ignore his entirely correct assessment, I mutter, "What do you want to do?"

"It's September," he says.

I wait.

Nothing more illuminates this obvious fact. It has been September for over a week, which means I *should* be debt-free right now. Unfortunately, the stupid loan company had me make an appointment for the end of September to see one of their representatives, so I am not. I murmur, "Yes… and?"

"Let's go to a pumpkin patch."

"What?"

"We can pick out pumpkins, then carve them, while drinking apt beverages."

My eyes narrow on the stupid canopy. I echo, "*Apt beverages?*"

"Pumpkin spice. Hot chocolate. Apple cider."

"Alcoholic?"

"Pardon?"

"Alcoholic cider? A little bourbon in that pumpkin stuff, perhaps? You know, there's a recipe for spiked hot chocolate I've wanted to try." I finish my fish. This disturbs me greatly. I wonder if there's more in the kitchen…

"Marcella…" F-man hesitates. "Do you have a problem we need to talk about?"

My brow rises. How does he know I just ran out of fish? Are there cameras in here? "What do you mean?"

"Things went somewhat oddly for you the last time I know you imbibed alcohol. It seems unusual that you'd want to prompt any similar situations. Especially in my direct presence. Unless you have a *problem*."

I know this man isn't suggesting I'm an alcoholic. "I've not drunk since my birthday, and before that, New Years. My only problem is that it sounds like you want me to go to a pumpkin patch, haul a giant orange thing home, then carve out its guts. I don't know how you expect me to do any of that without some sort of substance assist." I huff as my green beans also disappear. "Would it kill you to be a little less wholesome now and again? The proper response to my query is suggesting a drinking game where we take shots every time we see a pumpkin."

"We are going to see hundreds of pumpkins. We would die."

"Now who has the lousy sense of humor?" I mutter.

"Is there something else you'd like to do that won't have you resorting to alcohol?" he asks.

Shock therapy comes to mind. I don't say that though. "Pick me up at noon. Take me to get breakfast—"

"Breakfast? At noon?"

"I don't remember commissioning your opinion on the matter."

I hear a smile in his voice, but then again, when don't I? "Of course," he says. "My apologies. Continue."

"Take me to the pumpkin patch. We'll pick out pie pumpkins and carving pumpkins. While the pies are baking, I will watch you dig out pumpkin brains, then I will draw the face shapes I want in sharpie before I supervise you removing the designated locations."

"That..." He clears his throat, seeming almost breathless. "...that sounds amazing. Where would you like to get breakfast?"

"Taco Bell. They stop serving breakfast at ten forty-five, but I'm almost positive you can convince them to be more inclusive for those of us who stay up late playing solo Stardew. I've had this nagging desire to eat a Breakfast Crunchwrap past the appropriate time. Blame the rebel in me."

Tone much too warm for my liking, he says, "Perfect. I will see you at noon."

"I will be half awake and mildly interested in the planned activities."

"That's all I can ask for. Enjoy your time with Krobus, pumpkin."

Inexplicably, I blush.

And he leaves the call.

Chapter 12

Look up a video of a reticulated python eating a boar.

– Marcella

I think I've glitched.

I'm frozen in place, standing at the front door at exactly noon, staring at a modest bundle of purple, orange, and blue flowers wrapped in cream paper. It is impossible to drag my gaze off the square text on the card protruding from a plastic stick in the center.

On the one hand, how *dare* F-man be offering me a *Stardew Valley* bouquet in real life.

On the other, this man…this man who possesses all the money in the world…really has me pegged well enough to know that a handful of flowers with a cardstock-printed screen capture means more than something extravagant like all the gestures I see in fiction.

I blink, rub sleep from my eyes, discover I'm fully awake. My silly sleep-deprived brain has not fabricated this situation after eleven straight hours of Stardew, I guess.

What a dilemma.

"Do I need more heart events?" he asks, mildly sheepish.

Heaving a sigh, I reach for the bouquet, knowing I'm going to pull the card out and keep it forever in a little book with the pressed flowers. I can't believe him. I'm going to have to learn how to press flowers now. While anger threatens to take over, I nestle my nose against the soft petals.

Seriously…

The vibrant shades hide my smile.

How *dare* he.

I say, "I don't actually like watching flowers die, but this is an exception to that rule."

Sunshine explodes on F-man's face, eyes twinkling like oceans reflecting the blaze.

"I'm going to put these in water. Hang tight."

He is still blindingly chipper when I return. He rambles about how much he enjoyed playing Stardew with my friends and me last night while whichever bodyguard he has with him today drives us to Taco Bell. In a cruel twist of fate, the limo doesn't fit in the drive through, so we are forced to enter the building. At noon. On a Sunday.

As a practical celebrity.

Mothers battling toddlers stop to gape as we enter, flanked by large men in black. Polite as ever, F-man locks his hands behind his back and smiles at the menu listed over the register.

It occurs to me many moments too late that the menu is still listing breakfast.

Easing forward, I tug on F-man's sleeve. "Marshi, what did you do?"

"Hm?"

"It's twelve-ten. Why are the screens still on breakfast?"

"Oh." He beams down at me. "I made a call this morning and asked that breakfast be extended till one today. Or else."

He threatened a Taco Bell?

No.

That's a bit silly.

Arching a brow, I ask, "Or else what?"

"Or else I'd buy this franchise and adjust the breakfast times myself. But I really didn't want to go through the trouble of that and probably couldn't have had it done in time, so we came to an agreement that benefited us both."

Just a normal day in billionaire land, I suppose.

We get our meal to go, and I abuse his credit card by ordering myself the Cinnabon coffee, not the plain one. It's a dollar more expensive, and I'm disgusted with myself, but—at the same time—I'm not sure when I've ever been this happy.

Possibly when I found that Krobus elf mod.

The bar is terribly high.

After I finish the last bite of my cheesy, eggy, sausagey Crunchwrap, I say, "Thank you."

F-man looks up from his perfectly mundane, *non*-breakfast menu beefy five-layer burrito. He licks a bit of nacho cheese off his lip. "For what?"

"Going through the trouble of blessing me with this experience. I know you're rich, and that comes with an aptitude for shamelessness, but it's still very funny picturing you doing corporate talk with the franchise owner in order to extend breakfast for two hours. I appreciate it."

Warmth pours off him. "It wasn't any trouble."

"It required you to make a phone call. By yourself. As your assistant, I know the pain of having to call people. It's trouble. A *lot* of trouble. And someone makes it a necessity to call many, many people every time his little whims change his entire schedule…" My eyes narrow. "Accept my appreciation. It is in short supply."

"You're really driving home the *hate my job* thing. Most people don't mind working for me. I pay well, offer benefits, am a refreshing character to be around—or so I've been told."

"All true. And yet my aptitude for pessimism is remarkable. Why focus on the positive when the negative is more fun?"

"At least you're self-aware."

"One of my numerous virtues." I see a sign with giant pumpkins on it outside the window and realize we've managed to ease into the outskirts of the city. I sip my coffee and watch as a bustling sunlit field streams into view. Roughly a million children speckle between approximately a million pumpkins. And, in the distance beyond them, green stalks stretch to cover the horizon.

I gasp. "There's a corn maze."

F-man folds his wrapper against his thighs. "There is."

"Why didn't you tell me about the corn maze?"

His brows furrow. "I didn't think it would be of consequence."

My mouth falls open, and I stare at him as though he's *murdered* Krobus *right in front of me.*

"Do you…want to do the corn maze?"

"*Yes,* I want to do the corn maze. We are doing the corn maze. And *next time* there's a corn maze, you better tell me about the *corn maze.*"

Biting his lip to keep down a smile, he says, "I'll have my assistant make a note."

"Marcella. Put the snake down." Stiff and unsmiling, F-man maintains his distance as though I'm holding something venomous. "It's trying to bite you."

I point the little guy's primed open mouth at F-man. I have it by the neck and wrapped around my wrist, so it's physically unable to bite me. "So? It'll feel like a lizard bite. No big deal." I grin. "*Rawr.*"

Heat skates to F-man's cheeks. "I did think it odd you were so excited about a corn maze."

"Corn mazes are corn fields. Corn fields have corn snakes. Corn snakes are very pretty. I used to catch snakes and lizards and all sorts of things in the backyard with my dad. He'd always tell me I had to save as many critters as I could before he mowed the lawn, as though they wouldn't move out of the way." Petting the little snake's soft orange head, I chuckle. "Man, I was a dumb kid."

F-man inches toward me. "How do you know this is a corn snake?"

"Because it's a corn snake?" I judge him when he pokes the snake's body. "It's very obviously a corn snake. Have you never seen a corn snake before?"

"Not like this."

I tut. "What a sad childhood you must have had. Want to hold him before I put him back?"

To my surprise, he nods, so I carefully pass the teen noodle over, making sure F-man has a good grasp on its head as its body securely winds around his hand. They stare at one another for many pregnant moments. I don't think I've ever seen F-man more still, careful, or cautiously interested.

"It's pretty," he murmurs. "Do you know if it's a boy or a girl?"

I cross my arms. "I know you aren't asking me to look at this snake's butt."

The red in F-man's face heightens to a blaze as his attention lifts. "You can't tell by the coloration, like with birds?"

"'Fraid not. There are some size differences between male and female adults, but this is a teenager, and it's not a for sure thing anyway." Lifting its tail, I check its sex then murmur, "He's a little gentleman. If I could take him home, I'd give him a tiny top hat and bow tie, I would." The little guy opens his mouth to strike again when I try to pat his tiny head. "Mind your manners, little gentleman. We're not going to hurt you."

"Why can't you bring him home?"

"Huh?"

Painfully sincere, F-man says, "We can make a stop at a pet store and get him a cage if you want to keep him."

"First of all, we'd have to get him a *vivarium*. Not a *cage*. Second of all, wild snakes can have parasites. Not to mention that we're severely stressing him out just with this brief interaction. Oh yeah, and look at this." I throw my arm out at the corn stalks waving in the tepid breeze all around us. Sun dances off the yellow tassels and green leaves. "*All* of this is his house right now. It would be very mean to put him in even the best vivarium money can buy. No. I can't bring a wild snake home." I ease him out of F-man's hand and let him free at the base of a corn row. In moments, he's gone. "No snake for me. Goodbye, little gentleman."

"You know an awful lot about snakes," F-man comments as I start back the way we came.

"You should know more about snakes. It's important to value the animals that most people don't, like snakes, possums, and spiders… They're our front soldiers against a lot of pests that cause diseases. Even though so few people like them…they're working hard to keep the ecosystem in check. I appreciate what they do for us."

F-man watches me for several, silent moments—almost entranced—but as we pass his bodyguard sentries, he seems to forget we're having a very fun conversation. "Are we heading toward the entrance?"

"Yup."

109

"You don't want to finish the maze?"

I scoff. "Absolutely not. For most mazes if you follow one wall, you reach the end eventually. Which means it's just an exercise scam. I got my snake fix. Now, I require pie." Stopping in my tracks, I recall my manners and cast a look back at my for-all-intents-and-purposes *boyfriend*. "Unless…of course…you enjoy exercise scams and want to see if we can find more snakes up ahead? I mean, see if we can *reach the other side?*"

Chuckling, he shakes his head. "No, that's all right." When he makes it to my side, he splays his fingers near me. "May we hold hands on the way back?"

My lip involuntarily curls.

His expression warms. "I thought you might say that."

"I didn't *say* anything," I mutter. "Don't tell me my general disposition spoke for me? It has a habit of doing that. Rotten thing doesn't possess an inside voice."

He pulls a cloth out of his pocket. "Good thing I planned ahead."

I stare at him, then at the eggshell kerchief between his fingers. "Are you…going to cry?"

Twisting the cloth into a rope, he offers one end to me and smiles.

Yet again, my body reacts involuntarily as my heart bounces off my ribs. "You aren't serious."

"You don't want to be touched. I want to feel connected. Compromise."

It is a compromise. An excellent compromise.

Like, sincerely, it's a really wonderful and amazing compromise.

I can't believe he's actually going so far to meet me where I am.

Huh.

I grasp the other end of the cloth, look ahead, and

continue out of the maze.

Weird.

Chapter 13

No, I don't think I will.

– Finnegan

I'm uncertain what I expected *baking together* to look like. On the ride home from the pumpkin patch, while watching Marcella hum to herself and hug the carving pumpkin she picked out, I convinced myself today might continue to be a romantic experience.

After all, she accepted my compromise, and I deluded myself into thinking she was blushing as she did. Despite all my efforts, the fantasy came to an abrupt end five seconds after I dug the puree out of the three baking pumpkins we bought.

Before I could ask what the next step was, she banished me to the other side of the kitchen island, where she has only permitted me to mix the dry ingredients for the crust.

"They're beautiful," I say as Marcella trims the dough around the pie pans.

"Shut up." She gathers the scraps, rolls them into a ball, and tosses that ball to me. "Make yourself useful and turn this into little leaves."

My brow rises. I stare at the lump. My mother always rolled out the crust scraps, put cinnamon sugar on them, then gave them to Dad and me as snacks while we waited for her pies to finish baking, setting, or cooling. "You want me to make these into leaves?"

"Yes."

Okay then.

I insult all of creation with what I make, but Marcella places them on the smallest cooking tray in this place and...

She sprinkles them with cinnamon. And sugar.

Using a toothpick, she marks veins into the vaguely leaf-shaped mounds, magically correcting the disgrace of my abilities until they look somewhat lovely.

While the warm, spiced scent of pumpkin pie fills the kitchen, she tosses together the leftover puree with some apple cider we brought home, brings the mixture to a boil, stirs in an array of ginger, nutmeg, and cinnamon, then dumps ice into two tall glasses.

Once the concoction has cooled enough, she pours it over the ice and pushes one cup to me beside the finished collection of steaming cinnamon sugar leaves.

My heart squeezes.

When I don't move, she says, "Don't worry. I forgot to poison yours."

I close my fingers around the glass. "I'm not worried."

"Are you sure? You haven't smiled in the past ten minutes. In another ten, I'll have to take you to the hospital."

Light catches the glistening sugar just so, and nostalgia calls me.

"Marshi," Marcella states. "What's wrong?"

"It's been a while since I've done anything like this." Emotion riots, burning my throat the longer I fight to contain it. Wetting my lips, I take a sip of the drink, let the full-bodied blast of *autumn* sweep me up. "Do you..." I let myself breathe for a moment. "Do you ever miss something that you can't quite name until something else reminds you of it?"

She bites into a leaf and lets her attention drift off me. "Pirating movies with my brother."

I blink. "What?"

"It's what I remember when I think of things that I can remember but never experience again. We grew up poor. Really poor. Theaters were out of the question. Renting was a holiday luxury, and often the difference between being able to afford meals for the week or not. Sometimes, my brother would find garbage quality movies on all these terrible, sketchy sites. You could tell they were recorded on a phone in the back of a theater. Muffled audio. Out of frame." She laughs. "They were really awful."

"You...you have a brother?"

Her gaze finds mine, moves away. Lifting her drink, she leans back against the counter and focuses on the oven. "Had. He's dead to me." Her grip tightens around the glass. "Or...well...that's what I say, so it hurts less. He's kind of dead to everyone." She tilts her head toward the ceiling and closes her eyes. "Suicide."

A pit opens in my gut. "I'm so sorry."

Shaking her head, Marcella draws her glass to her lips, letting it rest there. "If you think I'm negative, he was something else. He could never quite see past each evening. Tomorrow simply wasn't a place that existed to him. We were so similar. But I figured out how to blend in when I needed to. I learned how to embrace who I was and ignore those who couldn't. I could turn my feelings off. He couldn't. He cared what everyone thought. All the time. And he lost his identity in trying to please everyone...in trying to be someone else...all the time. One day, he fell into the wrong group, took up the wrong persona...and... that was it."

114

All I can do is repeat a feeble, "I am so sorry."

She lifts a shoulder. "He was three years older. It happened while he was at college. And, like I said, I know how to turn my feelings off." She tosses a crooked smile back at me. "Mom was sobbing when she sat me down and told me what happened. I was so shocked, I immediately shut off. All I said was *that's a bummer.*" Biting her lip, she swears. Her eyes glass, but a cracking laugh leaves her. "No—" She swears again. "—wonder Mom thought I was a sociopath."

Abandoning my spot at the island counter, I circle the marble slab and wrap Marcella in a hug.

She tenses until I drag her tighter in against my chest.

After a moment, her face presses to my shirt. "What do you think you're doing?"

My voice breaks. "Nothing."

"There's a suspicious amount of *something* in this *nothing*, Marshi." She fumbles to set her glass down, but doesn't push me away when her hands slip up against my stomach. "Are you crying?" she mutters. "If you blow your nose in that hankie, I'm never touching it again."

"Thank you for the warning. I'll refrain from doing that then."

"I'm fine. Promise. You're the one who started this depressing topic. Which means I really should get you to a hospital…" Her hands close into fists against me, crammed hard between us, and it occurs to me that maybe she *can't* push away.

Because I'm crushing her.

I'm crushing her.

Loosening my grip, I gently run my fingers through her hair. She shudders and shoves, shaking me off with a grimace. "Don't ever do that again." Her attention rolls back to her drink while I recover from the loss. "So—" She

115

sips the spiced concoction. "—your turn to trauma dump. What did all this bring to mind for you?"

My mouth opens, but I can't wrap my mind around the words. If I dare say them aloud, they'll be too real. I'm not ready to admit I'm losing my mother. I'm not ready to admit...I've already lost most of her. I doubt I'll ever be ready.

"It has to do with your father, right?" Marcella prompts when the silence stretches. She swirls the liquid in her glass. "It's okay. You don't have to go into detail. A few years ago, I almost lost my dad to cancer. I don't even like to think about what could have happened." She huffs, glaring down at the cloudy, tan color in her glass. "The loan I took out to cover his surgery is why I'm in so much debt, but I'd do it again in a heartbeat because it saved him." Sneering into her cup, she mutters, "Just so you know, I'm *still* in debt to that dang loan company even though I have all the money. Can you believe it? Their office is on the other side of the city, so I went there on the first of the month with Bridge and my bill. Closed. Make an appointment. I spent over an hour on hold, but I was finally able to coordinate a date and time around the *end* of the month. I can't believe they're making it so difficult for me to give them thousands of dollars."

I can.

My brow furrows. "Who did you say you got the loan from?"

"I didn't."

"JustBorrow?" I ask.

Blood trickles from her face as her eyes widen. I don't need to explain a thing.

She curses.

"Yep," I mutter, crossing my arms.

"Is it a complete and utter scam?"

"Practically the mob." My jaw clenches. "They don't want you to ever be debt free. They rely on consistent payments, forever, from everyone they ever work with. A business partner of mine warned me about them."

Marcella swears again. "I'm an idiot. I mean, I knew it wasn't entirely safe, but I didn't think it was *organized crime*."

My head shakes. "You're not an idiot. You were desperate. And that's exactly what they prey on. Desperation."

"What do I do? Will they let me close my account with them at all?"

I smile. "They will, or I'll shut them down completely. Just tell me when your appointment is. I'll take care of everything else."

Chapter 14

For reasons I won't explain, you aren't allowed to take your ties off anymore.

– Marcella

"No, you listen to me. You're a *loan* company, aren't you? And your interest rates are listed clearly right here, aren't they? Which means this amount is the total due, isn't it?" F-man stabs a finger at the printed report of my loan, which includes the outrageous percentage these people sprung on me days after my initial *no interest for the first three months* expired.

A fission of warmth trails down my spine as I sit in a dingy office room beside F-man, flanked by nine of his bodyguards. They barely fit in the room, but given how creepy this place is, I'm so relieved they're here. Hands clasped in my lap, I watch my boss, my temporary boyfriend, a man I have only ever seen smile gently and kindly and considerately.

Right now, his smile *chills* me to the bone. It's all wicked promise. Venom. *Death threats.*

The man seated across from us fumbles through rules and regulations, claiming the terms and conditions I apparently agreed to, while he wipes a palm against his sweaty, receding hairline.

"I see." F-man leans back in his chair, drumming his fingers slowly against the wobbling desk separating us from JustBorrow's representative. "Let me make sure I understand: my client took out a loan with you, and she'd now like to pay it back in full. You are refusing to let her, despite agreeing that the amount she's offering is correct and compiles the initial loan with all incurred interest."

The man's eyes scan the *wall* of suits behind us. "I-I'm afraid there are fees and paperwork that need to process before we can accept a payment of this size. We recommend holding out another month and—"

"And incurring more interest, more fees, more headache?" A dry laugh exits F-man. He leans forward. "I don't think so. It's clear I understand perfectly what's going on. Now let's see if you do… I'm a businessman. I don't have time to waste. You work for businessmen, who I'm sure don't want to waste time handling this in court. Your higher ups have two options. Either they accept this amount, *today*, provide proof that Miss Keyes never has to speak to anyone here ever again, and leave it at that, or I go through the trouble of putting this place in the ground permanently. I don't care how long it'll take because I'm in the *fun* position of being able to hire someone else to deal with it."

"T-that's not necessary, sir."

"Excellent choice. In that case, *where's Miss Keyes's receipt?*"

When all F-man's bodyguards escort us out of the cramped building and back to the two limos taking up the entire parking lot, I'm so dazed—clutching the proof I'm debt-free—I barely register F-man slipping his hand into his suit pocket and murmuring, "Pumpkin?"

I drag myself from the fog of staring at the blurry words on the page I'm grasping. "Yes?"

His attention drifts across the cloudy sky. "Add decimating JustBorrow to my schedule."

My heart flutters. "Oh, um…" I push my hair over my ear, realize what I'm doing, and snap my arm back down to my side. "Yeah. You got it."

We slip into the back of our limo. Together. Just the two of us.

And, what do you know? It appears that in the time it took us to take care of this, I've developed claustrophobia.

"Where to, Mr. Marsh?" Mark asks through the small window separating the cab from the front seats.

F-man slides two fingers into the neck of his tie and *tugs*.

I jerk my attention out the window as my heart lunges for him.

No, no, no, no, no. I'm not. I can't be. Am I…?

There's a slight, slight, *slight* chance…I'm attracted to Mr. Marsh right now.

But who wouldn't be?

He just saved me from lifelong debt to a *mob*. From *never* being able to afford nice things. From perhaps always being reliant on him if I want a nice place to live…

I don't have to flush my money down the toilet anymore.

I'm free.

I am *free*.

I can build up a savings, plan for a future, *splurge* now and again without facing the crippling weight of poverty. When I move out of F-man's fancy mansion after all this nonsense is said and done, I'll be able to buy myself a proper set of Tupperware and stop using butter containers for my leftovers…

I'm not strong enough to resist a gesture that results in a future where I'll get to own *real* Tupperware. There's something primal about having dishes that fit perfectly inside one another. He's saved me, perhaps purely so I might enjoy that experience.

My mouth goes dry as I recall the last thing he said to me.

Add decimating JustBorrow to my schedule.

Since when does bright sunshine boy say words like *decimating*?

Heaven help me. I'm only flesh and bone. What am I supposed to do with the information that he wants to destroy something for *me*?

Hand trembling, I press my fingertips to my cheek and stare out the window at the winding back roads beyond a parking lot I will never have to see again.

I'll be bluntly honest… It is quite difficult to hate a man who wants to *destroy* things in my honor.

"Marcella?" he says.

My stomach flips, and I jolt my attention to him. His shirt. It's gaping. He took his tie off and unbuttoned his collar. "Mm?" I squeak.

He watches me for too many long moments. Right when I'm terrified he's seen through me, his usual gentle smile overtakes him. "You look like you're on the verge of tears. Are you that relieved?"

I look like I'm on the verge of tears? I have no idea what that looks like. I feel quite constipated. All the same, I say, "Yup."

"Let's celebrate with lunch. Where would you like to go?"

Lunch? With *him*? While his shirt is baring his chest for my innocent eyes to drink in?

No, no, no. I don't think so. There's no way I want to go anywhere calm and romantic with him while my emotions are this raw.

I need to fully remind myself that a brief snatch of something appealing does not make up for the rest of his character. It does not remedy all the things about him that I find mind-numbingly annoying. He is still an irritation to the nth degree. This simply does *not* make us compatible.

If only I weren't thinking about his hug in the kitchen a few days ago…

Surrounded by spices and warmth and *emotion*…

He smelled *so* good, and his arms for the first minute were solid enough to hold me together.

I enjoyed the first part of that experience far more than I am ever likely to admit.

Of course, then his overall *tenderness* ruined it, and he made me feel like there were bugs in my hair.

"Marcella…?" he prompts again, sugary sweet.

My lip curls as I regain myself. Ew. He's diabetes in a jar. A little well-placed destruction won't sway me. I am strong, and I am strong enough to resist.

"Food." My brows furrow. "Celebration food."

"Yes. Anywhere you'd like."

I think for a moment, then I say, "Sushi."

When his nose scrunches, I know I've made the right choice.

Normally when I get sushi, it's from this hole-in-the-wall place connected to a strip mall. Each roll—with like ten pieces or more—costs an average of five bucks. *Authentic* Japanese sushi isn't even available on the laminated menu. Which, nine times out of ten, is *sticky*.

This place…is not that place.

Soft, faintly oriental music flits through the air. Dim, romantic lighting floats above each table, gold-spun fixtures accenting gold-flecked décor. We're settled into a circle booth, in a far corner, distant enough I can't hear anyone else murmuring on the other side of the room.

My gaze catches on a single meal item costing forty-seven dollars, and I look away in lightheaded horror.

Come on, Marcella. You'll own a coordinated set of *Tupperware* someday soon... You can handle this.

I dare another peek.

I see a *vegetable dinner* with a whopping *three assorted veggies* that costs eighteen bucks.

Internally, I sob.

Whatever I order here is going to ruin me for my cheap sushi restaurant forever.

After the past few months, you'd think I'd be used to the extravagance of finding myself at nice restaurants or nice venues or in five-star hotel rooms, but something about the *customer service* façade places distance between whatever's going on and me.

It's professional dissociation.

Present enough to work. Absent enough to survive.

Basically, I remember nothing but a loose desire to murder everyone and everything within a five-mile radius.

Across from me, F-man's leg bounces under the table while his fingers drum against his leather menu. He's back to usual—smiling stupidly and moving excessively—but do I mind it less?

He doesn't like *sushi*.

That must reassure my hatred.

Sadly, it appears I have a soul, and after his heroic acts this day, it is very difficult to continue despising him for shallow things. Adding frustration to frustration...that leaves precious little to hate him for.

While I'm pretending to be the kind of adult who deserves nice Tupperware, I can admit it.

He's *not* a whiny manchild. If I weren't around to

handle his meals, he'd be buying and using his own three frying pans to reheat his food. He knows how to dress himself; I just eliminate the time and effort of coordinating his own outfits to match occasion and weather. My job is to free up his time. My job is to do the things he would otherwise do. He is neither unwilling nor incapable.

The decisions he makes that alter the schedules I've made are thought-out, effective, and meaningful. I know that because his businesses thrive. What he does *works*, and that's all that matters. So what if his actions give me more work and drag me around? That is *literally* my job description.

I'm honestly just pissy about having an amazing, well-paying, high-demand job.

I am a horrible, horrible person.

F-man runs his fingers through his auburn waves, rustling them so they catch new shades in the ambient lighting.

The only negative emotion I have left for him is envy.

I envy him.

I envy his easy smiles and his stable life.

There are so many struggles that can't touch him. So many struggles that built integral fears into the foundation of my character, forcing me to erect guards and walls. I don't believe that anyone exists without facing some kind of suffering, but there is a luxury in never waking up in the middle of the night to hear your parents worrying over how they'll feed their kids tomorrow. There is a luxury in never once believing you were a burden on the people you love just because you had to *eat*.

Loss comes for all of us, eventually, so while I do sympathize with his pain of losing his father so young, I can't pity him.

Outside the merciless flow of the universe itself, he is

untouchable.

And I envy that kind of safety.

Slowly, his gaze lifts, meets mine, and withers. "Marcella, what's wrong?"

I sniff, scorning the fancy cloth napkin because I'd feel bad blowing my nose into it. If I didn't want to not exactly hold hands with him again, I'd be demanding to see if he still has that stupid kerchief on him. Alas. Digging my fingers into my hair, I grip a fist at the base of my skull. "Nothing."

"There's a suspicious amount of something in that nothing, Marcella."

"I'm upset," I snap. "Being *upset* is my natural state. Ignore it."

"Is there anything I can do to help?"

Ugh. He's just *soo* helpful, isn't he? Flippantly, I nudge my menu. "Order me some sushi so I don't have to look at the prices and feel worse for taking advantage of you."

His brows rise. "Taking advantage of me?"

"What else would you call it?"

"We have an agreement."

A rueful laugh escapes me—half damp. "An *agreement* that leans heavily in my favor. Face it. No matter what happens, I get the better deal. You're too *nice* to be anything but perfectly amicable the whole way through." I swipe my free hand over my mouth. "*Why* did I agree to this?"

"Well, to be fair, I coerced you quite a bit."

"Yeah, because I'm a—" I swear. "—ingrate who was offered the chance of a lifetime and selfishly demanded more."

"Not wanting to immediately agree to marry someone you barely know with habits that annoy you isn't exactly selfish? Actually, not listening to your plea that I forget you applied was selfish of me."

"You *liked* me." Great. My voice is feeble and wobbly now. "You actually liked me. Not the person I mute and make tolerable. Not even the person I show to my friends. You liked the pieces of me that I only express when I'm alone. You've done so much for a chance to make my life a million times better, and I'm—"

He scoots around the circle booth, putting himself close enough to tug my hand out of my hair. Gripping it tight, he says, "You're scared, Marcella. *Scared*. And you have every right to be. I build up and tear down companies as though they're houses of cards. I hold all the power in this relationship. I control your job, and if I want to, your future."

"But—"

He silences me with a look that turns my bones to jelly. Soft, yet firm, he says, "But nothing. I've spent the past few weeks falling asleep while reading your answers to my form. I know so many bits and pieces of you from those words, and I feel such an inexplicable connection to who you are. You are used to being hurt, abandoned, ignored, and resented. For reasons you can't understand. So. You split yourself in two. You created a character who warranted no negative response, then you let the rest of your fragments embrace every cynical thought whenever you are allowed."

My eyes close.

He catches a teardrop on his thumb, swiping it off my cheek. "The hardest part about rejection is never knowing what in the world could possibly make you so…*wrong*. The hardest part about rejection is the marrow-deep understanding people find you unlovable…even when you've broken yourself into pieces trying to be loved."

I crumple, shoulders sagging, head drooping. I have no

words to explain how right he is. And, even if I did, I wouldn't want to share them—just in case I get it all... *wrong*.

He murmurs, "Did you ever get a chance to read my answers to the form questions?"

Numb, I shake my head. "I've been avoiding them. Out of spite."

He chuckles. "Well, after work today, I expect reviewing them to take up your evening."

My nose wrinkles. "Is that an order?"

Leaning forward, he plants a tickling, uncomfortably soft kiss to my forehead, then he whispers, "Yes."

Does removing my tie entice you, my dear?

– Finnegan

~~~

Absolutely go die in a hole.

– Marcella

Chapter 15

This means next to nothing, got it?

– Marcella

Mr. Marsh's words haunt me. Every answer to every question. And perhaps, especially, his answer to the last one.

Question 200: Why do you want to marry me?

I want to marry you because I believe it would be an honor to love you.

An honor.

To *love* me.

He's getting into my blood, and I don't know how I feel about it. Not one lousy bit.

Feelings are vulnerable, which is why I've not opted to employ any since deciding two friends was a perfectly reasonable number to have for the rest of my life. But feelings aren't just *vulnerable*. They're also complicated, and messy, and confusing.

They aren't safe.

They aren't secure.

And I desperately need security.

Not just financial security, either. If I only needed *that*, I'd be set.

So set.

I might be higher maintenance than I thought.

Even though I'm not as bad as Mr. Marsh's response to **Question 93: Do you consider yourself to be high maintenance?** which was: *Incredibly. I can't even eat peas and carrots in the same mouthful.*

As it turns out, neglecting to use your emotions leaves them somewhat frail and wimpy. Even without any scientific proof, I am convinced that emotions are a muscle, and mine have skipped every leg day since the beginning of time.

Taking a deep breath, I touch the pumpkin charm on the necklace I decided to wear today, grip my LeoPad a little tighter, and knock on Mr. Marsh's office door.

"Come in," he calls, his smooth, warm voice too much for me to handle right now.

My head does terrible things with the tenor, morphing it into new words then playing those words on repeat in my skull: *I believe it would be an honor to love you, an honor to love you, an honor to love you.*

The thunder in my chest makes it marvelously hard to breathe as I enter and find him looking intently at his computer screen while twisting in his chair.

I think I've been too resentful to realize… He's always at work before I am.

He puts in more hours than he asks me to.

"What do we have today, Marcella?" he murmurs, flicking his attention toward me and smiling. His smile fades when he catches sight of my necklace. Even though I dug around in the fish tank muck for the missing charm for over an hour, I have not worn this silly thing since that first day.

As a protest.

Obviously.

I say, "You have a Zoom meeting this afternoon, at

two."

"My asset management team?"

"Yes."

He nods once, eyes never leaving my necklace. "You'll take notes?"

"I will."

Resting his chin in his hand, he lets a bit of his smile return. "What else?"

"Several designs and brand updates need your approval. Your PR manager wanted to talk to you about a few interview opportunities for next month. And—" Wow. This is actually physically painful. "—I've decided to handle all the planning myself, so I was wondering if you preferred an indoor or outdoor wedding, Finn."

He stops twisting his chair as his gaze jumps up to my face and his lips part.

When he snaps his mouth closed, red slashes across his skin.

Catching his affliction, I turn on my heel and clap my hand to my mouth. Because I may very well puke.

"Did you just say my—"

"No!" I blurt, choking on pride, embarrassment, *the piece of pumpkin pie I snitched on my way out the door this morning*. Even knowing *full well* I'd have to order breakfast minutes after getting here. "That never happened. You're hallucinating." Battling the incessant beat of my heart, I say, "What do you want for breakfast?"

"You."

My organs give out.

I chance a glance back at...*Finn*, find him looking hopelessly handsome, and forget how to breathe for longer than is wholly recommended. I wish with every atom in me that he'd start clicking his pen and make me hate him all over again.

130

He does not oblige.

At long last, I take in a breath I don't know I'm withholding, wet my lips, and force down a swallow.

Finn threads his fingers together and props his chin in the canopy. "I take it something in my answers resonated with you?"

Every last word felt like coming home.

Every last answer was a love letter responding to my own.

His words were stable. Funny. Endearing. They reflected a thoroughness I'm addicted to. In them, I felt understood.

Seen.

Wanted.

I'm so scared I could cry and hit things.

Finn melts a little in on himself, murmuring, "Well, if you aren't on the menu, I guess I'll have an onion bagel with egg, bacon, and cheese. Deconstructed. Butter on the side."

What a metaphor.

Despite absolutely, one thousand percent *not* being on the menu, I'm feeling somewhat deconstructed myself. "Anything to drink?"

"Pumpkin spice latte. Hot."

Why does that sound like an innuendo?

Why do I feel in over my head?

I have regrets.

Immediate, soul-sucking regrets.

"Marcella."

It hurts to breathe when I find him watching me with something very close to *adoration* on his face.

"You're okay, dear. Remember. I like *you*. I'll never ask you to force yourself to do anything you don't want to. There are no hidden expectations to meet. You simply

131

fascinate me, and I enjoy having you around in any capacity you're comfortable with."

That's a real cute thing to say. Shame I don't know how to handle it.

Pouting at my tablet, I pull up *Finn's* favorite bagel shop to put his egregious order in. "I wish you'd be meaner to me. I don't know what to do with nice people."

His smile tilts into darker shades. "You wish I'd be meaner to you?"

"I know you're incapable. It's fine. I'll get over it. Maybe with persistence, I'll learn how to function in a healthy relationship."

He exhales a laugh. "That is the goal."

"My goal is actually to corrupt you first."

"Just so I'm clear on your wishes, could you explain what being mean to you looks like? Open communication is very important to me, and I would hate to overstep in my efforts."

He's so *family Christian pure* I might gag. If only I weren't looking at beautiful pictures of bagels and deciding which I want to put on his card, as girlfriend tax, not an employee meal. While I am still an employee and my meals are still tax write offs, I am busy *reframing* how I consider my boss. Girlfriend tax is simple: when the boyfriend eats, the girlfriend does, too.

Lest she take to devouring him under the light of a full moon with nothing but a steak knife and her bare hands…

Mm.

Weird.

I'm not certain *Finn* could handle what I mean when I say *be mean to me*. The periodic mandatory death threat just does not seem to align with his TV Y-rated MO.

Ignoring his query, I mutter, "I can't believe you're making me order from two separate locations for your meal and drink. This is abuse."

"Oh good. Abuse sounds like I'm succeeding in the *mean to you* department. Should I add a dessert from a third location, or is that too far? Would it make you utilize the safe word? *Or* does the safe word exist as a safeguard against the potential of going too far, allowing me to live freely and only step back once I hear it?"

Internally, I scree. Swallowing against the mutiny of my heart, I order *myself* a custard doughnut from a third location, tack a pumpkin spice doughnut on for boyfriend tax—because, yes, it goes both ways—and press my tablet to my chest when I'm done. "You appear rather competent at teasing, which is not easier on my feeble nerves. Please treat me with utmost disregard if you are incapable of meanness."

"So, to you, teasing and being mean aren't synonymous?" He tilts his head to the side.

"*Teasing* is flirty and clever. Being mean is…" I puff a breath and look away. This is really going to sound messed up. "You know. Like. Bullying. No pleases and thank yous or smiles and kindnesses. Only insults. Undermines. Disgusted expressions. Pretending I am a crumpled rag housing a crushed bug. Show me I'm the absolute *opposite* of a burden on you by how little you give a crap about me."

"Marcella."

Face red, I meet his gaze. "What?"

"Can you weave taking you to therapy into my schedule?"

I scoff and turn on my heel. "I'm going to go wait for our food!"

"Marcella."

Stopping dead in my tracks, I refuse to turn around—especially given that he's found a pen to click, which is about to make me rabid.

With all the gentle force of a train, he says, "You are the absolute opposite of a burden already. The fact lies in your job description. You know, in case you needed that reminder. My life is, quite literally and quantifiably, easier with you in it. Okay?"

My chest squeezes, and I can't justify that with a response, so I just nod before I step out.

Awful lot of something in your next to nothing, pumpkin.

– Finnegan

Chapter 16

Pleasure doing business with you, Mrs. Marsh Industries.

– Finnegan

"No."

I sigh, holding the pad and pen out as Marcella, a notary, and I bump along in the back of a hay-filled trailer. "Please?"

Her angry eyes jet my way. Arms crossed, she huffs. "Absolutely not. Also, for the record, *who does this*?"

"Does what?"

Marcella tosses a hand toward Margo, the notary, who is patiently waiting with her stamp to confirm Marcella's signature. Then she sweeps her arms to reference the entirety of the hay ride I organized for us to go on after work today.

"I told you I wanted to go on a hay ride." I click the pen shut, then open, then shut.

Marcella's pretty brown eyes narrow into slits. "You know something, Marshi?"

I stop clicking for a moment. "It takes you five business days to work up the nerve to call me by my first name just once?"

Her arms snap back together, impertinent. "You are an incurable tease."

"Glad you noticed. Now." I tilt the pen toward her. "One signature gets you on. One signature gets you off. There's no risk to you, and it will help me to no longer need to confirm purchases or transfer funds into the executive assistant account while you plan our wedding. If it weren't so easily reversed, I'd accept your wishes. But, for all intents and purposes, it is painless, and leveling the field between us going forward is important to me."

"You are insane if you think I won't go mad with power the second I have access to all your money."

"I truly hope you do go mad with power. I'm awful at redistributing the wealth to the working-class since most of my purchases are from business-related corporations or fall to large-scale charity organizations."

Marcella angles herself away from me. "What if I mess up and cause the collapse of Marsh Industries?"

"Then you are more skilled than I thought. No single purchase could come close to toppling the empire. Not even if the single purchase is a several-million dollar home."

"What about *several* several-million dollar homes? I might lose my mind and buy vacation spots in half a dozen countries. How much does an island cost? What about developing it? How much will it cost to build a tiny hobbit hole island paradise with carrot fields and wild pet rabbits whose only cage is the surrounding ocean?" Her fingers dig into her bicep. "This started as an exaggeration, but now I will need the cost estimates and a list of available islands."

I sigh. "My grandfather already bought an island before he died. I haven't even been there, so you're welcome to develop it and fill it with pet rabbits as it suits you. Rabbits aren't expensive and neither is building a modest hobbit home."

Her head whips my way. "You are—" She swears. "—joking."

"Why would I joke about that?"

Wary, she looks between my face and the pen I'm clicking. "What's my monthly budget? At least give me a monthly budget."

"No. No monthly budget."

"I need something to ease my *you're going to mess up and ruin everything* anxiety. I'm not a *proper* rich person. I will be scrolling through Instagram, ordering anything cute I see, randomly donating to Kickstarters, buying up my *entire* Steam wish list in preparation for when Stardew Valley removes its claws from my jugular, and I need other farming sims." She slaps a hand to her mouth. "I'll need to buy a *gaming computer.*"

"You will. You also need to decorate your home so it's less like a generic magazine and more...*you.*"

Her chin lifts, adorably arrogant. "I'll get rid of all the beds."

"Please also stop sleeping on the couch. Honestly, your aversion to change is commendable, but I fear for thirty-year-old you's back."

"You are making an awful lot of demands this fine evening, *Finn.*"

I bite my lip to mute my smile. The way she said it sounded like a curse, but this is the second time she's said my name. It fills me with such incomprehensible joy.

An idea hits me. "Actually."

She tenses.

"You do have a budget. I expect no less than half a million dollars to be spent every month."

"*What?* How do you expect me to spend half a million dollars *every* month? That's six *million* dollars a year! I've never even seen *a hundred thousand* in the flesh. I save butter containers to use for my leftovers!"

I watch her.

Something in her seems to connect the dots. Clearing her throat, she adjusts her position. "I'm starting to see where I'm less than a concern..."

"Mm, yeah." I push the papers toward her and tap the pen against them. "It really is good to put money into the kinds of places you want to support, pumpkin. It helps the economy. And not having extra wedding-related purchases to confirm frees up my time. No longer needing to send funds to the exec card does, too. Financially securing you against me is just one of the many pros to this move. It's important to me that you have that stability as you transition into truly considering having me as your partner."

She drinks down a deep breath and scowls. "Ugh." Snatching the pen, she calls to the driver, "Stop the tractor. I don't want my signature to be bumpy."

Sitting in the middle of an overgrown field on bales of hay, I watch Marcella sign herself into my world. The sunset rays caress the black ink as she finishes every initial and date before passing the sheets to Margo.

My heart rate picks up when she releases a breath, clenches her hands against her thighs, stretches her fingers, clenches them again. She whispers a curse, laser-focused on Margo as the woman signs, dates, and stamps the appropriate locations.

Margo briefly relays how my bank will set Marcella up with a username and password before issuing new cards for her while my poor girlfriend has a tiny, almost imperceptible breakdown. The only way I can tell she's having a breakdown is because she's started smiling and nodding politely.

Throughout the ride back to drop Margo off near her car with the paperwork so she can begin processing it, Marcella remains quiet—blank.

Once the tractor is taking us back out into the field

beneath the twilight, she whispers, "I'm...rich." She clutches a hand to her chest. "How do you live with the weight of this responsibility?"

"You get used to it."

"I may require a lobotomy for that." Starkly horrified, she turns her face toward me. "And guess what? *I can now afford it.*"

"Realizing I'm powerless to stop you is an odd sensation. I wonder if physical apprehension might be sufficient."

A deep, villainous laugh starts deep in her chest. She steeples her fingers together, tapping them in tandem. "I must use this power for *evil.*" She stops herself, drops her hands, and corrects the mischief in her expression. Fixing me with a glare, she says, "See? I'm already going *insane.* What have you done?"

It takes everything in me to keep my laughter in check. "Could you describe what you mean by *evil*? Please? I am painfully curious."

"I don't have to tell you *nothing.* I can quit my job, find your island, and begin construction of my hobbit home. This is it." Her gaze drifts heavenward, and her brown eyes glitter in the stardust. "I've completed the main storyline. I've unlocked Ginger Island. I have the funds to repair the boat in the back of Willy's shop. I'll buy the supplies from Robin directly. I don't even have to gather them."

"I hardly have a clue what you're saying."

She flaps a hand at me. "*Stardew Valley.* You're still too early game to understand. And we really should remedy that." She gasps, again, eyes so wide I'm worried she'll hurt herself. "Once I have a card, I should take you out."

My face heats. "What?"

"On a date. To celebrate my richness. Stealing the bill when the waiter hands it to you sounds very fun."

My lips part.

She arches a brow. "What? Did you think I meant I was hiring an assassin?" All blood rushes from her cheeks. "I can afford an assassin." She grasps aimlessly at the hem of my long-sleeve shirt. "I...think I need to lie down."

Without warning, her head hits my lap, and I choke on my heart when it lodges itself in my throat.

Vaguely unfocused, Marcella stares at the sky. Distantly breathy, she whispers, "Finn?"

I speak around the beat in my esophagus. "Yes?"

"Do you know any good assassins?"

"Why do you need to know?"

"Why wasn't that answer a *no*?"

Oops. Right. "No, sorry. I don't know any assassins. I can't say I've ever ordered a hit on anyone."

"Well, that's boring." Her lip juts.

She's...precious.

My hand lifts, but she snaps, "Touch my hair and die. *Literally*. I will hire people to find me an assassin and then I will hire that assassin."

I dig my fingers into the hay at my side.

Her eyes close.

I lose all sense of self, watching her.

A shallow sigh slips from her lips before she murmurs, "I'm still getting my bread off the discount cart. Walmart doesn't need your money."

"True, but a small local bakery might. Just imagine. Fresh *in-date* bread."

"I resent every word you just said."

I bury my hand deeper in the hay, let it prick my palm. "Sorry."

"Mostly on account of your correctness. I'm rich now. I get to be pretentious and shop at farmer's markets. What will I do with my love of bread cart now?"

140

"I don't...think shopping at a farmer's market is pretentious."

"Whole Foods? Earthfare? Fresh Market?"

I let my tongue roam my cheek. "All perfectly normal locations that regular people often shop. They could not be supported on rich people alone."

"I've got it. A private health food co-op. Where you need a membership card to enter the building and old ladies provide unsolicited information about how honey isn't vegan, so they only ever use *agave nectar*, while you search for your almond flour and sesame snacks."

"Pumpkin."

Her eyes open to find mine.

"You're my assistant. You know where a billionaire shops. You do my shopping for me."

She blinks. "Oh. Right. You have me order through Marsh Delivers Fresh. You narcissist."

"Back when my father launched the grocery delivery service, I wanted to name it MarshMallow."

She snorts. "How dare he crush your creativity."

"Indeed. My genius has been squandered since my youth. It would have had a little logo with the double M's, which is the sound you make when something is delicious."

Another laugh escapes her. "You're so..." She sighs and turns her attention back to the sky. After several moments, she says, "Don't stare at me."

"Sorry." I also tilt my head to take in the sky. Out here, far enough from the city lights, the sky is a tapestry of glittering jewels that sprawl on and on into places money can't hope to afford.

Not looking makes the weight of Marcella's head in my lap far more present. With every bump and shift, I find it harder to breathe.

"MarshMallow," she whispers into the growing

141

darkness. "That should have been your Stardew name."

"It carries too many bitter memories."

"Is that a joke, or should I apologize?"

"It's a joke."

The most palpably dry and forced chain of laughs ever leaves her. "Your dreams were crushed. So funny."

Her sarcastic laughter shouldn't be able to incite something real. Unfortunately, it does, and I cave a little bit over her, unable to restrain myself.

"Hey," she protests. "That sunshine is blocking out my night sky." She pokes me in the nose. "Where's the dimmer on this thing?"

I catch her hand before she can stab me with her nail again. Despite the calm of this moment, a hay ride isn't the most smooth, and I'm not eager to lose an eye.

"Finn?" she says when I've gone too still, perhaps when I've drifted too close, certainly moments after I've begun thinking of the technical difficulties involved when it comes to kissing her in this sort of position. My stomach flutters at the sound of my name on her lips. Again.

It's the fourth time.

I'm almost certain I'll lose my entire soul come the fifth.

"Yes?" It takes everything to keep breath entering my lungs.

"Would you like to go home and play *Stardew Valley* with the girls?"

I smile and try not to mourn the loss when she pulls her hand free. "Nothing would make me happier."

Except, perhaps, marrying you.

Chapter 17

These schemes spark joy. Get it? *Spark?*

– Marcella

"You're an awful boyfriend," I say, riding home with Finn from a dinner meeting. I'm in my assistant garb, despite his threat that I'd be attending these boring things as his *date* at some point in the future. My relief knows no bounds as I have zero interest in being someone his boring partners and business bros feel obligated to talk to.

Finn's brows rise. "I am?"

"Yes." No. He's the best boyfriend I've ever had. Although, to be fair, every other guy I've ever gone out with was more a *single date* sort of thing, less an *official boyfriend* one, which would make him the *only* boyfriend I've ever had. Therefore, he is simultaneously the best, and the worst.

Relaxing with his arm propped on the car door, he plants his chin in his hand and does that thing where he loosens his tie and pops the first button of his dress shirt. "Does this have anything to do with my insistence that bullying you seems unethical?"

"No, but now it does. Keep adding crimes, and I'll have to take a vacation to my island."

"Would you like to honeymoon there?"

143

My back straightens, and I look up off my tablet. I was organizing notes from the business dinner. Now, I don't remember a thing about it. I'm almost positive watching Finn take his food apart didn't bother me as much as normal—because he ordered an appetizer just for me and I was too busy counting to thirty before taking each piece, so others had time to share with me if they wanted. Even though no one did. Man, I ate that entire thing by myself, didn't I?

Maybe I should have counted to a minute each time. Or…started counting *after* I swallowed.

"I can have it refurbished to look like Ginger Island by the end of November," he murmurs, all…*sultry*…and *loose-tied*. "We can spend our time planting crops, fishing, cooking…"

"But can you put in a volcano and fill it with monsters for me to attack?"

His gaze drifts, considering. "I'm not certain I want to give you a sword."

"Wow. A third thing to add to my *awful boyfriend* essay."

"Lovely. A Baconian. I look forward to reading it."

I set my LeoPad down beside me, lace my fingers together, and lean forward. "Finnegan."

A touch of heat crosses his cheeks. "Yes, dear?"

"What day is it?"

"I'll have to check with my assistant. All I know is it's not the weekend, else I'd be playing Stardew with my darling girlfriend and her friends."

Head shaking, I fiddle with my pumpkin necklace—a habit I've developed since I started wearing it each day. "Your assistant says it is October 7."

"Ah, October 7, then. It has been getting cooler. The leaves will change soon. Fall is wholly upon us. Apple

144

picking season. Shall we make plans for more pies soon?"

He seems overly eager. He must've really enjoyed making pumpkin pies last month. "You disappoint me."

"I know. I lie awake at night attempting to locate a cure for that specific and raging condition. Thus far, my efforts are coming up fruitless. My final resort is to take a class on Bullying 101, but the semester has already started, so…" He catches sight of my stern expression, and the humored tilt to his lips settles. "Is this a serious thing?"

"Of course."

"Truly?"

"Not even a little bit."

He relaxes. "Please elaborate."

Sighing dramatically, I lean back, cross my arms, and look out the window. "It's *October 7*. Which means it is not between May and September. Do you know why this is relevant, or do you hate me?"

His mouth opens, and many thoughts flicker through his blue eyes. Finally, he says, "Is there a third option?"

"No."

He murmurs a swear. "Marcella, you know I'm quite entirely useless without you. Is the information you're looking for in any of the memos you send me? On my schedule, perhaps? We started dating in late August, so it can't be a three month anniversary I missed."

"For the record, you don't need to celebrate every month-iversary. That is weird. And goes beyond the amount of privilege I am able to tolerate."

He splays his fingers over his mouth, entirely pensive. "Marcella," he states, "I must earn my good boyfriend points *somehow*."

"An entire eighty dollar Publix cake every month is not the way."

"You don't like watching flowers die. And jewelry all

145

the time is too generic. And you weren't all that fond of my forcing you to buy so many clothes…"

"You can figure it out. No more cakes. No more *anything.* For a few months. At least. I'm all gifted out, and I have access to all your money now, so if I want something enough, I'll get it myself."

His lip juts, and he plants his fist against his cheek. "When are you going to want something, exactly? I'm still waiting on that one."

"Three nights ago, I bought a pizza with the card connected to your account. I bought *two*, actually. Plus bread sticks. And a soda. *And* I had them delivered to the house. So I even paid the delivery fee. Even though I not only had food at home, but I *also* had a Teresa who would have made me food if I'd asked. Or if I texted you to ask for me. Because I have a mental block where it concerns asking people to do things for me like that, and you, clearly, do not."

"The sixty-two dollar charge has broken me, I promise you."

"We are off topic."

He smiles. It's blinding, per usual. "May I have a hint as to what the topic is?"

I fill my lungs with so much air in order to release it all in a judgmental sigh. "The weather is cooling. The Summer Burn Ban has lifted."

"Bonfire," he says. "You want a bonfire."

Letting my lips pinch, I stare at him. "I'm actually very offended you caught on so quickly. You were supposed to be clueless until the last second."

"I'm so sorry, my dear. It has been seven entire days since we could be legally burning things in mass outdoors." He splays his fingers against his face, grieving. "I have utterly failed you."

I sniff. "See? Now you're getting it."

"Is it a good time to tell you that I've been planning a bonfire since you mentioned it, and I already have a list of things we probably need that you can consider or merge with whatever plans you have?"

My haughty act falters. "You..." I press my lips together and scan him from the tips of his pretty hair down his scandalously open shirt. "Are giant pallets on the list? So we can stack them all up? And then set them on fire?"

"I was going to box stack oak logs."

"That feels more legal than burning pallets. Hence, I'm less of a fan."

"How big do you want this fire to be?"

"How tall are you?"

"Six-four."

My brows rise. Okay. Dang. "Yes."

A tender smile flirts with his lips. "Are you thinking about pushing me into the flames?"

"No, I'm thinking about having a smaller fire so I won't be scared to get close while roasting marshmallows." I pick my tablet up again. "Can I access your list from here?"

He unbuckles his seat belt, crosses the cab and slips into the spot beside me before directing me to the correct location on my tablet. He's thought of everything. Drinks, snacks, seven types of marshmallows. The chocolate fountain is almost as excessive as the presence of fairy lights in the cart, but the picture every item on the list pulls together is perfect.

We can set up between the pool and the butterfly garden. Run extension cords out there. Hook my music up to surround-sound speakers.

It's much too extravagant for the few guests I was thinking of.

"Finn."

"Hm?" His murmur hums near my ear, and I realize he's close. Very close. But he's not touching me.

And I don't know if I've appreciated anything more.

Looking at him, I say, "Not to be mean, but do you have any actual friends?"

He doesn't flinch. "No."

Yikes. Poor boy.

I say, "My guest list is really short. This seems like a lot of effort for less than ten people."

"I prefer your friends to anyone I could invite."

"Right...but still." It's not a *bonfire* unless you have at least a couple people you can sacrifice, and I'd be reluctant to lose anyone on my current list.

Finn rests his head back against the seat. "If you'd like, you can open it to friends of friends. Let Penny and Brigid invite some people they know, too. And you grew up here, didn't you?"

"Yeah?"

"Invite your parents."

I bristle. "My *parents*? I haven't even *told* my parents I've moved into a mansion. I do not want to put you in the same room with them."

His gaze cuts to me, amused. "I must put my foot down on the bonfire being *outside*, pumpkin. No rooms included in the event."

I scoff. "I meant the same *vicinity*. And you know it. I was distracted by the stupidity of your idea and resorted to the cliché. What, are you also planning to invite your mom or something?"

His tongue swipes across his bottom lip before he pulls it between his teeth and looks elsewhere. "No. It's not exactly her thing."

"So who would my parents talk to?"

"The friends they invite?"

148

Oh. Yeah. I forgot about that.

It would be an awful lot of explaining to do.

But...I mean...talk about *fun*.

A whole, real party with all the people I like and all the people they like.

In my backyard.

With *fire*.

I've never much fit in at or enjoyed parties before. The ones I've had to accompany Finn to were pretentious and crystalline. The idea of a party that doesn't make me feel adrift in an endless sea of confusion sounds too good to be true.

This one will happen in my backyard, which I'm very familiar with given how often I've sat outside with my butterfly friends since moving. I will get to choose my own music, and change it at will. The guests will include my friends. The refreshments will be solely stuff I like.

It will be beautiful.

With the single recipe for disaster being this man in a space with my mom and dad...

But, all things considered, if by some miracle I go through with the insanity *next month*, my parents should probably meet...my boyfriend...*before* seeing him at my *wedding*.

"Does it sound like a plan?" Finn asks.

Swallowing abject terror, I nod. "Absolutely. I can't wait to leave a circle of ashes in your pretty lawn..."

"Two," he says.

I raise a brow at his perfect, calm smile.

He lifts his fingers to count. "One bonfire, one marshmallow fire. Two circles of ashes. Twice the burning enjoyment. Double happy girlfriend." His smile turns a bit stupid, and a bit dear. "*Best* boyfriend ever."

My eyes roll off him, and I huff, but I can't stop myself

from smiling at my tablet as I scroll through the cart he put together. Just for me.

Ha ha ha. You're hilarious.

– Finnegan

~~~

Don't patronize me.

– Marcella

Chapter 18

I have you on benefits. Your insurance covers therapy.

– Finnegan

"Pumpkin," I call as I wander toward her bedroom. Penny and some men I hired are busy outside, setting up the final things for the bonfire, which—last I checked—was an exceedingly tall blaze just far enough from the house to not singe the shingles. People will begin arriving any minute now.

Marcella's door is open by the time I reach it, and my heart thumps upon witnessing the sight beyond the archway.

She's standing in front of the floor-length mirror on the wall beside the closet. A cream and brown dress we bought in August hugs her curves. The loose long sleeves billow to her wrists while the skirt flares with each of her slight turns. Unlike her usual modest makeup, tonight she's wearing an obvious orange and gold dusting of eye shadow that matches her pumpkin necklace.

When she looks at me, I am convinced.

She was made for autumn.

Her skin, hair, and eyes all reflect the brilliance of the season, and I don't know what I'll do once I see her bathed in the gleam of firelight.

Tonight might kill me.

But at least I'll die happy.

"What?" she says, and I remember myself.

Lifting my phone, I say, "One of the playlists you sent me to get hooked up to the audio…"

"What about it?" She wanders to the dresser and gets a hair clip that's laying beside the engagement ring I gave her after our first date. I'm surprised she didn't toss the ring in a drawer somewhere out of spite. As it stands, her pillow and blanket are still laid out on the couch in the center of the room.

I clear my throat and try not to stare at the ring. "It's called *Probs Need Therapy*?"

"Every song on it is a total bop. Can confirm."

Every song on it is a depressing nightmare.

"I'm…sure." I checked the lyrics of some. I can't say anything about the tunes right now, but the cry for the tomb was disturbingly apparent. "Are you sure you want me to shuffle these into the music for tonight? Your parents will be here soon."

"Finn." Her head lops to the side, and her straight, short hair caresses her neck in such a way I'm left breathless. "They raised me, honey. I think they can handle it."

"Honey?" I echo.

"That wasn't an endearment. That was the southern *bless your heart* intonation. It's the *oh, you poor dear, your parents simply never bequeathed any brain cells to you in the will, did they?*"

I watch her. Longer than I should. The bold makeup is throwing me almost as much as how thick she just laid on her southern accent. Seeing her in this dress outside of the store has me ready to drop to my knees. She's beautiful. Stunning. Gorgeous.

It's shocking that I wasn't in love with her at first sight

during her interview for the position of my assistant. I guess her plastic airs and strictly professional attitude, on top of her presentation concerning how intricately she would manage my schedule, was too distracting.

"Are you good?" she asks. "*Everyone* will be here soon. Teresa will be buzzing guests in for us, but I think we're supposed to greet them." She lets a pretty little smile soften her features. "How's this look for *gentlewomanly host*?"

"Lovely."

"You'd never suspect I'm thinking about sacrificing any of the people I don't know personally, right?" Her lashes flutter. Angelic.

I offer her my arm. "My dear, you can afford all kinds of therapy now. Your incredible insurance doesn't even need to cover it. Just use your shiny new card."

"Finn?" she murmurs, surprisingly tucking her hand at the crook of my elbow. Sweetly gazing up at me, she says, "I'm so glad we stacked the pallets up to six-five." Stretching, she taps the top of my hair. "A little extra room for the quiff."

Laughing as I pocket my phone, I shake my head—and, apparently, my *quiff*. "I'd hardly notice if you burned me alive. It feels like I'm on fire every time I'm with you."

"All the pain without the charred reward. No brittle bones for my soup." She pokes me in the arm, loses her *good host* expression, and scrunches her nose. "I bet you'd be too sinewy. Chewy. Will need to slow cook. Mm, yes. No charring for you. 'Twould be a waste."

Should I be concerned?

Nah.

This is fine.

Probably.

Once Marcella's done pretending she's going to boil me alive until the muscle falls off my bones, we head outside

153

where she splits off to help Penny sample the display of chocolate fountain treats while I get the music started.

To Marcella's credit, she was absolutely correct. The lyrics leave me worried, but her songs are definitely "bops."

As I'm debating grabbing a chair by the smaller marshmallow-roasting fire to wait out the influx of guests, the first vehicle pulls up. A tall man wearing glasses steps from the driver's side while a woman smaller than Marcella with long straight hair exits from the passenger's. The woman pins me immediately and marches while the man trails along behind her, both hands in his pockets.

"Marshi."

I recognize the voice instantly. "Brigid. Nice to formally meet you."

"You're taller than I thought you'd be."

She's shorter than I thought she'd be. Her consistent no-nonsense tone even when she's joking on our Discord calls seems as though it shouldn't quite fit into such a petite frame. Then again, all Marcella's anger doesn't seem like it should fit inside her body, either.

The man catches up, his gaze drifting over the strings of hung fairy lights designating the party area between the pool and the butterfly garden.

Brigid smacks him in the stomach. "This is my husband, Cody. He likes sports, snakes, and when I put my feet against his back in the dead of winter. Become friends."

She's gone before I blink, streaking across the lawn toward Marcella, and Penny, who appears to have fifteen marshmallows in her mouth.

I hum. "Well, it feels like I'm in middle school again, being forced to hang out with the kids of my parents' friends." I extend my hand. "Finnegan Marsh. Nice to meet

154

you, Cody."

"Likewise." He takes my hand, shakes it once, then stuffs his back in his pocket. "I don't suppose I need to explain that I know nothing about sports and don't much care for snakes?"

"What about the cold feet?"

Something gentle touches the firm line of Cody's mouth as his attention homes in on his wife. "A necessary evil."

As it turns out, Cody likes stars. He met Marcella during an astronomy elective in college. She introduced him to Brigid when her friends came to visit, and the rest was history. He fell hard and fast, so before Brigid could head home, he asked for her number.

They made long-distance work for three years.

Then he moved to be with her.

It's almost jarring to hear how simple it's supposed to be. No bribery. No forms. Even if I weren't in the position I am, I don't think I could do it.

I like knowing too much about my investments before I take a chance on them. I doubt I'd ever be able to make such a lifelong decision without analyzing the risk before feelings could get involved. I've always believed that relationships feel too much like shady business deals.

With people, you never know what you might expect, who you can trust. You either outline your expectations in excruciating detail, thus confining your relationship to terms and conditions, or you prepare to be hurt.

The rare exceptions so far have been my parents...and now Marcella.

Despite our contractual agreement and her position as my assistant, the only terms are that she's obligated to be herself and treat me as she would treat a significant other. Shunning that law almost entirely, she's blunt about her needs and her limitations, treating me with the most honesty anyone ever has. I don't have to guess about whether or not I can trust her even when I have no idea what she's going to do or say next.

The woman's a wild card in a flawlessly stacked deck.

As dry and calculative as she is, it's hard not to fall in love with her.

She…

It hits me halfway through Cody pointing out how Jupiter should be rising in the next few hours.

He's going on about the visibility of the planets throughout the night and into the morning, but my attention is squarely on Marcella. In her pretty dress. With her glittering makeup catching firelight.

She's talking with an older couple I assume to be her parents.

She's eating a marshmallow she just finished roasting.

And I…

I've been thinking about her this whole time.

I've been thinking about *how hard it is not to fall in love with her* this whole time.

As though I'm not already head over heels.

Chapter 19

You're lying.

– Marcella

"You are a disgrace to humankind," I murmur as Finn catches his marshmallow on fire.

Puffing, he blows it out and presents the terrible blackened glob. "It's the fastest way to cook them."

"If I would break up with a normal boyfriend over this, do I get to break up with you?" I turn my own marshmallow above the flickering flames of the little fire while the big fire blazes a short distance away. Right now, only Finn and I have gravitated to the little flames. Most everyone else—including my parents—have begun slow dancing to the string of gentle songs in the clearing beside the bonfire.

I am desperately waiting for something like "Bullet" by Hollywood Undead to come on and shake things up.

The friend-of-a-friend tactic worked to pack the entire, vast space between the pool and the butterfly garden with people and laughter. This entire night, I've been thinking so *this* is why people like parties.

I don't think I've ever genuinely smiled so much before in my life.

By the time my marshmallow has cooked through, I

pull it off the skewer and pass the glorious golden brown delicacy to Finn.

Brows raised, he leans back in his camp chair and looks at my meager offering.

"You'll never cook a marshmallow in under seven minutes again. This will ruin you for all other options. This...*this* is the only correct way to roast a marshmallow. And if you don't agree, I'm sorry, but we are over."

He chuckles as he slips the marshmallow from my fingers. "No pressure, right?" He takes a bite, and surprise knocks the smile off his face.

Mmmhm.

Many a fool have I toppled where my method of roasting is concerned.

My mother used to think a marshmallow was done when it turned *golden brown*.

Ha.

Noob.

"Marshmallows expand when they cook. If you want a raw marshmallow, okay fine. *But* if you want it *cooked* over a *fire*? It needs to be warmed all the way through. The question is: how can you tell it has been? Well, easy. They expand when heated, so it'll grow to approximately twice the size of a raw marshmallow." I snuggle up in my camping chair, smug. "Marshmallow science."

"This is the best marshmallow I have ever had. I can't believe you broke down how to achieve an optimal roast."

I shrug. "When you grow up poor, one bag of marshmallows is a nutrient-free luxury. You take great care in deducing how to achieve the most deliciousness out of roasting them over a stove top."

"Most kids wouldn't give it that much thought, I think."

"Most kids would try and catch their marshmallow on fire as though setting it directly on the hot coils wouldn't result in a sticky, horrible mess. I'm *special*."

Finn's soft smile returns. "Let me guess. You're describing the behaviors of your brother?"

"I am absolutely describing the behaviors of my brother." I snort. "Man. He was such an idiot sometimes…" I rally another marshmallow for death and begin the tedious, constant process of turning it for half a decade just out of reach of the flames. "I was, too, obviously, but I'm only admitting it because he can't speak up for himself." I glance at the dancing couples, the food, the lights, and the roaring bonfire. "I wonder if he would have loved this as much as I do. It was really hard to tell when he enjoyed something if he wasn't inclined to tell you. He was a skilled pessimist, and some people are really good at sucking the joy out of everything." I give my head a shake and turn my attention back to my marshmallow. "Like me. Right now. Talking about my dead brother at a party. Hi. How are you? Having fun? Saw you talking to Cody earlier. And then my parents. I was busy hiding and sobbing into my potato chips, of course, but I hope that went well for you. I'm sure I'll hear more about it later, but Mom did already beam a *Mom look of approval* across the yard at me while I was crying. So congrats on that."

Finn finishes the marshmallow, eyeing me like I'm a puzzle he's lost the rest of the pieces to. He's busy searching under my couch cushions and card table, hoping the dog hasn't absconded with anything important. At last, he says, "For the record, I don't mind when you talk about your brother. Knowing that you feel comfortable doing so means a lot to me."

I scoff. "Don't think it means anything. I'm a diagnosed oversharer. Many an unsuspecting fool has been blessed with the knowledge of my dead brother. I once told a bank teller while I was setting up an account in one of those fancy back rooms. She stood up from her desk and hugged me. It is still singularly the worst thing that has ever happened to me in my life."

Finn coughs, hiding a laugh, as though he has to, as though I don't see all his sunny sweetness *constantly*.

I mutter, "Please tell me what happened between you and my parents."

Biting his lip, he lets his gaze drift skyward. "Well…"

Dread swells in my gut. I cannot imagine why.

"You already briefed them on everything, from our dating arrangement to the fact you're on all my accounts. Your father did his due diligence in assuring me no number of bodyguards would stop him from taking me down if I hurt you. Your mother apologized for him. And then she apologized for you. Said you were an *odd* one. Always had been."

I shrink, just a smidge, and stare at my cooking marshmallow. It's getting where it needs to. Yay.

"Then she promised me not a one of my bodyguards would find my remains if I took advantage of that. So I dare say the compulsion to provide me with death threats runs in the family."

Something in my chest eases as I laugh. "You know something? It really makes sense that it's a genetic trait."

"Does it now?" Finn watches me while I pull my marshmallow off the prongs and take a bite. Caution coats him, and he circles his fingertip around the plastic of the cup holder in his chair's armrest. "Marcella."

I arch a brow.

"I…" He clears his throat. "Well, could you… Would." He swallows. "Would you…"

"Are you having a stroke?" I ask.

He blurts, "Would you tolerate a dance with me?"

A laugh bursts from the very deepest part of my chest

with such force I nearly lose my marshmallow.

Finn nods, gripping his armrest. "Right. Yes. That's what I thought. Never mind."

Stuffing the rest of my marshmallow in my mouth, I let my nose wrinkle. "Come on." I set my skewer down by my chair, take his hand, and drag him away from the blaze, the people, the fairy light circle. I bring him to the butterfly garden, guide him through the arches of flowers that will soon frost away. Pausing at the switch for the fountain lights, I turn on the bubbling centerpiece so an ice blue glow coats the scene.

Beyond the cover of blossoming trees, bushes, and extravagant archways, music, crackles, and voices drift.

"Okay." I face Finn once we've reached the most spacious swathe of grass in between the benches and flowers, beside the fountain's bubbling gleam. "Pay attention. Here's what you're *not* going to do."

He stands straight, stiff, stunned smile-less.

I graze his cheek, barely touching, with my fingertips. "Feel that?"

He chokes on the word. "Yes."

"I hate that. The there but not there sensation *sucks*. Any touch I'm not expecting *sucks*, so always give me a heads up if I can't see what you're doing, then…" I grip the back of his neck, letting my nails nip into the base of his skull. "…then make sure you follow through. Be assertive and definite. Don't worry about hurting me because the soft crap actually hurts worse. If that makes any sense to you at all."

In the white-blue light of the fountain, he turns compelling shades of red.

"Are you comfortable with what I'm asking for?" I murmur.

"You…want me to be rough with you." His lungs fill.

"Are you comfortable with the intimacy of that request?"

My heart flutters. I search his eyes. "I don't know. Let's find out."

Before I drop my hand, he grips my wrist, plants it solidly against his shoulder, and scrapes his fingers down my arm, through the long sleeve of my dress. Reaching my waist, he reels me in, hips against his, every finger present through the fabric of my skirt. He takes my free hand in his other. Ballroom style.

I don't get a moment to laugh and remind him that the extent of my *dancing* skills begin and end with *lamely sway*. He bends my fingers back, stretches my pulse, and presses a hard kiss to the beat.

It leaps against his lips.

"Marcella," he says. His eyes meet mine, torment and desire thick in the darkening blue.

I lose all the feeling in my legs, but he has me. Completely.

When his fingers find my hair, they bury deep and grip fast, baring my throat. A disgraceful sound I'm refusing to dwell on strangles from my mouth.

He dips me, letting gravity pour my weight into his hands. His damp breath runs across my cheek, and I don't hate it. I *don't*. Not even a little.

Voice gravelly, he whispers, "May I kiss you?"

Scalding warmth boils beneath my flesh, burning every spot our bodies connect.

He's got me off balance. Dizzy. Helpless.

I did not at all think he meant *this* kind of dance.

All I can say is, "I've...never been kissed before."

He tugs on my hair, and I think I lose my soul to him. "My dear." He nips at my bottom lip. "That was not a *no*."

It most definitely was not.

Both my hands skim up his chest, around his neck, and

into his auburn locks. I lift myself to his mouth against the pull of his hand in my hair. As our lips connect, urgency consumes the action, pressing his warmth into my body, into my veins. My nerves erupt.

He controls me, guides me, pushes me back until I collapse against one of the benches in front of the fountain. The hard wood bites into my spine as his fingers dive from my hip to my knee, dragging a sensation of presence all the way down my thigh. I swear. He swallows the word.

When he pulls as far back as I'll let him—which isn't so far at all—I catch the most beautiful sight I have ever seen.

He's tousled. Wrinkled. On his knees before me. My skirt is flared and pressing to his jacket as my legs rest around him in a sort of scandalous manner I don't want to think about.

Flushed, lips parted, he scans my position in relation to his body, from my awkward posture to his grip on my leg. Then…he *smiles*. Dragging me by my knee against the seat until I'm on the edge, he catches my entire jaw in his palm and *looms* over me. "That's my girl."

A shock zips straight through my chest, frying my nerve endings.

I have *never*, not *once*, been *anyone's* girl. Ever.

But, right now, I think his assessment is one hundred percent correct…

Moving back, he jerks me fully onto his lap in the grass. The wood presses into my wing bones as both his hands take my wrists prisoner.

He's stable. Commanding. Assured.

Everything I think I've always wanted.

When his fingers slip around mine and clutch, I tremble. When he whispers, "I really like you, Marcella," I tense.

It is so very, very hard to breathe. "I…would hope so. After all this."

"I want a life with you."

My stomach clenches.

"I don't mind figuring out what that looks like so you can be happy. I don't mind learning how to fulfill what you need. You destroy me, Marcella." He kisses my cheek, hard. "Teach me how to love you."

A shudder pours down my spine, and I lose all the feeling in my body. Pressed—completely—against him like this, I can hardly hear my own thoughts above the hammer of our hearts singing together.

Hoarse, I say, "What haven't you given me, Finn? What more could I ask for from you?" I wet my swollen lips. "You aren't the one who needs to be taught anything else if we're going to work out. I am."

His head tilts. "Are you saying you're happy with me? Just as I am?"

I swallow, averting my eyes. "I…don't know. At the very least I'm saying you've put in every effort to meet me where I am, when I haven't even bothered trying to appreciate it."

"I don't like how you talk about yourself sometimes, pumpkin."

"With honesty?"

"It's not honest." Releasing one hand, he hooks a finger in my necklace, then he yanks my face to his. "Being guarded isn't the same as dismissing me entirely. Countless times over these past few months, I've challenged you, and you've conceded when you've agreed that I was correct. You aren't stubborn. You aren't difficult. You aren't *emotionless*. You have given me every grace when you have felt safe enough to do so. You are allowed to withhold your emotions concerning me until you feel safe to experience them."

I might cry.

I really don't want to.

Lip quivering, I whisper, "But I *am* stubborn. I'm *still* sleeping on the couch when there's something like seventeen beds available."

The corners of his mouth soften. "You're not stubborn. You're spiteful. There's a difference. And the proof is that you'll agree with me in a moment."

I sniffle.

He swipes a thumb beneath my eye, plants his palm firm to my cheek, and drags his short nails against my skull to push my hair back from my face. "Am I wrong?"

My head shakes. "No." I cave against him, squeezing his hand for strength. "You're right."

His arms close around me, tucking me so perfectly against his body. "I love you," he whispers into my hair.

My heartbeat stumbles.

"I love so much of you. I'd like the opportunity to love you more each day. I'd like you to love me, too, but I never want your love to mean sacrificing any part of who you are. I want an eternity where you tell me anything that's on your mind without fear I'll reject you. I want you to snap at me if I'm twisting my chair too much. I want you to scoff and leave the room when you can't stand being around me. But I always, *always* want you to come back when you're ready. No matter how long it takes. I want to know, with complete certainty, that you spend the time with me that you do because you enjoy it. I know you're happy by yourself. I know you're capable of so much without me. So…all I'd like is if you could love me enough to choose to be around me every so often when perhaps you would have been just as happy alone. I'd like you to love me enough to choose my arms over anyone else's when you need someone who knows how to hold you the way you want to be held. I'd like you to love me." He pauses, and his fist closes against my back, crushing me so tight it's almost painful. But it's completely...*completely* perfect. "I'd like you to love me...because, Marcella, if you love me *at all*, it will be more than enough."

My muscles shake as I fight for my every breath, battling to keep the rush of tears pouring down my cheeks silent.

In a single, crashing wave, it's all *too much*.

I shove myself out of his arms, tripping as I fight to get on my feet.

I can't *breathe*.

I can't *think*.

Looking down at him—kneeling, arms open as though awaiting my return—I *can't*.

I'm shaking.

I'm frozen through.

My fingers hurt when I try to close them into my palms.

My mouth opens, and I attempt to find a reply that he deserves, something to reassure him that it's okay, he's okay, I'm okay; however, I *can't* right at this moment, for some reason.

All I can do is knock on the top of his head with my knuckles, turn sharply, and flee.

I want nothing more than to throw myself into the bonfire as I pass, but as I march away from him, through the crowd, and past the tall flames, I refrain. I refrain until the party dies out, and I refrain until I fall asleep, yet again, on the *couch*.

Chapter 20

I'm not.

– Finnegan

"Are we gonna talk ab—" I begin, staring at Marcella.

"No. We aren't going to talk about anything. Tonight is not a night for discussion. It is a night for bad decisions. The worst ones we can find, actually. I expect you to respect that." Gaze planted on the city streaming by, she uncrosses her ankles to cross them in the other direction.

It's been a week of pretending what happened at the bonfire doesn't exist. A week of *business as usual*.

Every time I close my eyes, she's on my lap. I taste her with my every swallow. I *feel* her. In my hands. On my skin. Throughout my soul.

When she fled the butterfly garden, I maintained the strangest sense of calm as my fingers threaded into my hair where she—almost lovingly—conked me on the head. As the fire died and everyone went home, I waited for the peace to break. I spent the first few days after the experience expecting a panic attack or a breakdown.

Some undeniable feeling I had ruined everything.

But Marcella came to work like normal. She talked with me like normal. She rolled her eyes and prodded and scoffed like normal. For about a week, we have been completely *normal*.

Then, last night, she sent me a picture to a sold-out Halloween event with the single command: *Make it happen.*

And now?

Now she's a butterfly goddess.

It doesn't at all escape me that this woman purchased her costume over a week ago but only sent me the flyer yesterday. However, I seem to have lost the ability to mind.

She's ethereal. Massive blue wings pour behind her. The cape ties to her middle fingers, letting the reams of fabric move with her every motion. Her makeup is extravagant, oceans of blue, white, and black. Her short dress leaves room to display thigh-high black tights, and the low-cut neckline means the pumpkin charm she's fiddling with rests against her bare skin.

The woman is a vision.

And I am severely under-dressed in a pair of khakis with a green jacket.

"I want a candy apple," she murmurs. "But I don't want to bite into a candy apple." Her face turns toward me. "You know?"

"It is an inconvenient and sticky sort of battle."

She returns to peering out the window, murmuring aimlessly, "I hope they have caramel apple funnel cake."

"What exactly is this place we're going to? I made the appropriate phone calls, but I didn't exactly research."

Her gaze skids toward me. Then back out the window. "It's some kind of fair. But scary. There's a haunted path that takes you through a dilapidated cabin and into the woods while actors with chainsaws and axes may or may not chase you. But before all that, there's a spooky little town with food and souvenirs. A couple rides, I think." Pulling her hand from her necklace, she closes her fingers together against the frills of her skirt. "I do not anticipate having a good time. I expect it will be quite crowded. And loud. And have dozens of people paid to grab at the guests."

"Is there any specific reason you wanted to do this?"

"Yep."

She provides no further information as the sprawling parking lot for this *Halloween town* comes into view. A team in safety vests directs us to a parking spot, then Mark and Jeff open the doors for us. Marcella spills out in a flurry of her wings while I step out. In my slacks and jacket. Like a loser who did not think to prepare for dressing up on Halloween, and then did not expect his unpredictable girlfriend to do so, either.

Even from all the way out here, the creepy airs of the town entrance and whistling music sends a chill down my spine.

Beyond bag check, neon flashing lights and smoke screens obscure storefronts. Cackling actresses dressed as witches lure people into their shops. A cauldron bubbles in one corner, and the woman seated before it appears to have a fake rat tied to her finger so she can continuously pretend to throw it in.

My heart hits the roof of my mouth when Marcella's small hand wraps around mine. Our fingers thread as her grip tightens, and her nails prick my skin. Already when I look down at her, she seems to be in pain. Lowering my head near her ear, I say, "We don't have to be here. You can tell me what you want out of this and wait in the limo while I get it."

Her head shakes, then she tugs me into the fray.

"Come, dearie." A witch intercepts us, mangled fingers beckoning. "Come, try a potion. Finest brew on the street." She presents the colorful bottles filling the window behind

169

her. "Anything your heart desires, right here…for a price."

"Are they alcoholic?" Marcella asks.

"Ah…" The witch clears her throat. "…no."

"Pity." She points at the display, at a pink flask clearly labeled *love potion*. "What flavor is that one?"

"Drop of care. Pinch of cinnamon. Strawberry ambrosia. And a *dash* of lust."

Marcella, unamused, hums. "Does it come in a pretty bottle or a plastic cup?"

Both. Apparently. It comes in a little bottle with a cork and two labels—one designating that it is a love potion, the other warning that it is *not* edible. Then it also comes as a fruity soda in a plastic cup.

Marcella gets both, listens to the witch ramble about how we must share the concoction in order to effectively cast the spell, then promptly pockets the inedible trinket before taking her sip of the drink and passing me the cup. "Bibbidi-bobbidi-boo."

I don't get a taste.

"Wait a second." She pulls the cup back and looks in at the faintly bubbling fluid. "This is actually really good. Sorry, Finn. You need to get your own." Uncharacteristically chipper, she takes another sip.

"You're supposed to share for the spell to work." I remind her and reach for the cup. "One sip, for the spell, then you can have the rest."

She turns her back on me. "No. Mine."

"Pumpkin—"

She slurps. "I know what's happened… I've fallen in love with this drink! You tricked me, you nasty witch."

Playing along, the actress cackles.

Marcella murmurs, "I may die of a broken heart once I'm done. Woe is me." *Slurp*.

I can't tame my smile as I order a drink for myself, and

a third to share, which Marcella only accepts because I get a sip in before she can wrestle the cup out of my hands.

We meander in and out of shops, on the hunt for something apple flavored with caramel.

Unfortunately, there is a shocking lack of such things. But we give it the best shot we can by stopping anywhere offering food and sampling the menus. As we're sitting in a gothic, bone-themed cafe, Marcella freezes with her brownie halfway to her lips.

"What is it?" I ask, cutting into my tart.

"What you picked looks good."

I chuckle, cut a bite, and hold my fork out across the table. "If you like it, I'll get you one."

Heat crosses her cheeks, but she accepts the offered morsel, licking a bit of the custard off her lip. "You'll spoil me completely, acting like this."

"I'm not remotely concerned. I bet you spoil like a fine wine."

"Hm…" Without looking, she holds her brownie out to me. So soft I can barely hear her beneath the eerie music pouring from crackling speakers all around, she says, "Is this…what forever would feel like?"

Mouth full of chocolate, I stare at her. Managing to swallow, I reply, "What does this feel like?"

Her gaze startles to me, then she shoves the whole rest of her brownie in her mouth and does not reply.

Chapter 21

Yes. This is what forever will feel like. I promise.

– Finnegan

Marcella nestles against me while I try not to break the spell. No doubt that love potion worked…but I'm terrified it will wear off before I'm ready. It's late. A midnight hum buzzes in my ears as she sits beside me in the limo, curled up on the seat, head in my lap. Making sure to apply consistent pressure, I rub her shoulder and flick through photos of the evening in my mind.

She survived three minutes on the haunted path. The second a man with a chainsaw actually did appear, she stabbed her finger at him, barked *no*, and latched onto my hand. While Mark and Jeff fell in to protect their princess, she marched me back out into the streets, to the cafe, and downed another brownie.

Because I ate a bite of hers the first time.

And she quite entirely required a whole one.

Shortly after that, she told me she was done.

So now we're here.

Going home.

It feels like I'm trapped in a dream that just escaped the atmosphere of a splendid nightmare.

"Finn?"

My hand stills against her shoulder. "Yes, love?"

"It's November."

Breath tightens in my lungs.

November.

Thirty days until the wedding.

Thirty days until I get to see what all the purchases and planning and brief, nonsensical sorts of questions she's asked me throughout the past weeks add up to.

Thirty days left for her to decide whether or not she wants me to be her husband, or whether she wants me to go back to being just her boss.

Maybe her friend.

Hopefully her friend…

I might be too reliant on playing *Stardew Valley* with her each weekend to go back to being *just her boss*. I have chickens that I've named. I need to pet them every day. It's imperative I see a pixel heart rise above their heads even though Brigid insists there's an *auto-petter* I can get to avoid the experience.

I'd hire an assistant before letting a robot take care of my sweet baby hens…

Okay, yes. I hear it, the flicker of madness. It's obvious, but—plainly put—I don't know what I'd do if I had to give up the world Marcella has shown me.

"Can we go apple picking next weekend?" Marcella murmurs, sleepy. "I want to bake another pie. And make a deconstructed candy apple so it's not a pain to eat." She yawns. "I've never made funnel cake before… The apple options at that horror story were pitiful…and I did so have my heart set on caramel apple funnel cake."

I squeeze her arm. "I adore everything you just said."

The smallest smile eases over her face as she reaches to grasp my hand. "I'll let you stir the dry ingredients again. Maybe you can peel the apples, too. With one of those fancy machines that makes the skin into one long string. Apple noodle skin snake snacks for me."

I am going to make her the best apple noodle skin snakes I possibly can.

Practically asleep now, she whispers a curse. "I need to coordinate a time when Mom, Bridge, and Penny can come wedding dress shopping with me. I'm not looking forward to that. But I did find an appropriate boutique relatively close." She steals my hand completely when she rolls onto her back, looking up at me. "You have no friends, so I've asked Mark and Jeff to be your groomsmen."

"What?"

"They've already been fitted for their suits. Would you like Cody to be your best man?"

My mouth opens, but she doesn't let me respond. "You don't actually get a choice. Since my two friends and Mom will be my bridesmaids, you need three people on your side, too."

Of course. That makes perfect sense. How silly of me to think such a question wasn't rhetorical. "Do you need me to ask him, or have you already?"

"I've told Bridge that you will ask him soon. He already knows, though, because he also already has his suit. The asking part is a formality, to solidify your broship."

Chuckling, I smile, say, "Touching your head," and make sure my nails reach her scalp when I comb my fingers through her hair.

Her eyes half-lid before they close and she snuggles my arm, pressing my fingers into the crook of her neck.

"Pumpkin?"

"Mm?"

"I could have sworn you weren't this affectionate."

She bites my finger.

I think my heart skips a beat on its way into her palm.

174

Planting a little kiss over the bite mark, she murmurs, "I'm touch averse, which means I'm touch starved. Congratulations." Her eyes open—deep and dark and hopelessly beautiful. "You now know how to touch me in such a way I don't feel the primal need to perform an autopsy."

"That's—" I clear my throat. "—great. Really great."

"I had fun tonight."

"Me, too."

"In unrelated news, I never want to do this again." Her eyes narrow. "*Unless* you buy all the tickets, and tell them to turn the flashing lights and smoke machines off. Also, confiscate the chainsaws. And maybe everyone can wear nice clothes instead of witchy outfits. It wouldn't hurt the shops to clean themselves up and opt for more of a cottagecore vibe, either. Turn the whole thing into a fairy butterfly garden for just the two of us."

"I'll see if I can contact someone willing to sell the love potion recipe."

She gasps, sparkling. "You get me." Her smile erodes, and she scrunches her nose before biting the whole fleshy part of my thumb. "I mean, no you don't. Shut up."

I melt into a useless puddle. In a lapse of judgment, I twist her hand into my grip, pull it up to my mouth, and bite her back.

Her eyes widen.

"What?" I murmur against her knuckles.

Streetlight streams in the windows to catch on her blushing cheeks. "Nothing..." She settles, and her eyes close again. "Nothing at all."

Awful lot of *something* in that *nothing*, but I let it slide.

By the time we make it back to her place, it's past one in the morning. A quiet stillness fills the chilled air, and Marcella's bundled up in her wings for warmth as she flutters up the steps to the front doors. Breath puffs from her mouth when she yawns. "You have two bodyguards in the car," she murmurs into the sleepy cold.

My brow arches. I tilt a look back at the car, picture Mark and Jeff chatting beyond the black-out windows. "Yes?"

"Pity."

"Pity? Why?"

She opens a front door and peeks into the gaping dark lobby. "What would they do all night if I invited you in…"

My lungs constrict so violently I think I might be having a heart attack. Swallowing, hard, I fight to contain myself and say, "My dear…what would *we* do all night if you invited me in?"

"Sleep."

This information doesn't cease my heart's efforts to beat from my chest.

Lingering in the doorway, Marcella frowns back at me. "If you smile, I'll stab you, got it?"

I train my expression fully neutral and nod.

She takes a fortifying breath, releases it into the void that is the dark lobby, then mutters, "I'm…scared. Tonight was an absolutely awful decision, and I don't want to cry myself to sleep with the lights on."

My lips part.

She's scared.

She's scared and she wants *me* with her.

I'm awestruck, dissolving, happier than I should be, when she lands the final blow: "Besides—" She flicks nonexistent dust off her skirt. "—whether or not I can stand sharing a bed with you is valuable information for the future."

"We don't have to share a bed if we get married," I blurt. "Our bedroom will be large enough to have separate beds. Or, if even that bothers you, you can have your own room."

"Finn." She glares at me over her shoulder. "Don't you think you're a little *too* accommodating? What's the point of getting married if we go on to act like roommates?"

Helpless, I say, "B-because...I love you."

Heat races up her neck. She cuts her fingers into her hair and digs her nails into her scalp. "Go take care of Mark and Jeff. I'm not walking through this pit of darkness by myself."

After I let Mark and Jeff know that they can head home for the night, I escort Marcella to her bedroom, take off my jacket, and try not to fall apart when she leaves the bathroom in one of the pairs of pajamas she got from Walmart. She gives me a firm once-over while brushing her teeth, then mutters through the foam, "I don't think any of my clothes will fit you." Turning to spit in the sink, she sighs. "I guess you'll have to sleep in your boxers. Assuming you wear boxers. Anything less than boxers, and I *will* cry."

While my brain derails on a blinding image of that experience, I remember a vital detail.

This is my house.

I have a bedroom here.

With *clothes* in it.

By the time I've changed into a pair of flannel pants and a plain t-shirt, Marcella has snuggled herself into the bed with the pillow that was previously on the couch.

"Well," I murmur, bracing a shoulder against the wall and folding my arms, "isn't this a momentous occasion?"

Her brow knits, and she points to the foot of the bed. "Guard dogs sleep there."

Chuckling, I make my way to her bedside.

She tugs the blankets up around her chin as she sinks

down. "What are you doing?"

"Goodnight kiss?"

Her eyes search mine as she covers her mouth with the comforter. When her head shakes, I oblige, banishing myself to the other side of the bed. Firmly so. It's a big bed, so there are roughly two feet of modest space between us.

It is nowhere near large enough to get swimming thoughts out of my head.

Everything in me burns to close the distance. To crush her to my chest. To inhale the scent of her hair with my every breath. I want to let her scald my lungs and tease my flesh with her barest movements.

Instead of doing that, though, I flatten my hand against the clean, cool sheets between us and stare at the canopy above when she uses the remote on her nightstand to turn off the main light.

The room goes pitch.

I hear her shift when she rolls over.

It kills me not knowing whether she's faced toward or away from me.

"Marcella?"

"What?"

Toward, then. I close my eyes and let out a breath. "Nothing. Goodnight."

Silent moments pass. Weariness creeps up on me. It has been a long day followed by a long evening. That town really was creepy in all kinds of ways, which was a precedent set well in advance. Why in the world did Marcella want to go at all if she can't handle scary things to such an extent she's asked me to stay with her tonight?

I could ask.

The worst she can do is tell me to shut up and go to sleep.

That's one of the many beautiful things about Marcella.

I don't need to question anything with her. She'll tell me what she's thinking without sparing any frills. She is just genuinely simple to be with.

The sheets rustle, then her fingertips graze mine.

I latch onto her hand without any prompting, and murmur, "Yes, love?"

Her swallow echos in the darkness. "You…were too far away to properly protect me from the chainsaw murderer assuredly hiding under the bed right this second."

I smile. "This is delightfully unexpected behavior on every front."

"I don't know what you're talking about. I'm demure and feminine and soft. All the time. Without any exceptions."

She is crushing the life from my hand.

Not that I care.

She wriggles closer, and I don't know how my heart is going to handle this for much longer.

Her free hand plants on my bare arm, rushes up, and pushes my shirt onto my shoulder. "Wearing short sleeves?" she whispers. "Big mistake." Her teeth clamp into my bicep.

I can't stop my laugh or my swear. Unfamiliar feelings go rippling through my veins. "Okay. *Okay.* What is with all the biting?"

Her lips smack as she nuzzles. "Boyfriends are delicious. I don't make the rules. Don't tell me it bothers you?"

"Just wondering if you're taste testing for when you slow-cook me."

"I absolutely am doing that. Got a problem with it?" Her foot finds mine. If I'm not mistaken, her toes are very adeptly pulling my flannel pajama pants up my calf. I can only imagine why.

"I don't have any problems with it. I may like it a little too much, given our pre-marital status at present."

Her freezing toes burrow under my knee once my pajamas can no longer protect me.

Cupping my free hand to my mouth, I turn my face away from her in an effort to contain my bliss.

I adore her. I adore her. I adore her. I adore her. I adore her.

Her fingers dip beneath my shirt, against my abs, and I have to catch her hand then. Breathless, I whisper, "Please. If you're coming on to me...say so now."

Her forehead rests against my shoulder. "It's dark..." Painfully soft, she says, "I'm...trying to hug you." A small breath runs against my arm. "For warmth and survival purposes only."

"Of course. What other purposes are there?"

"I don't know. Surely not any illicit ones."

"Surely not." I tug her arm and trap her in my embrace. It's not my fault she winds up partially on top of me, her weight indenting itself in my mind for all eternity.

After all.

It's *dark*.

Her hand fists in my shirt. "You're not a very squishy pillow, Finn."

"Am I more comfortable than the couch?"

"No."

I sigh, and she rises and falls on top of me. "My apologies. What do I even have to offer to this relationship?"

She plants a kiss to my chest, through my shirt, and—tenderly—says, "Financial security."

I murmur, "I suppose that's valuable in this economy."

"'Tis."

I'm not entirely sure when our meaningless

conversation ceases to be words. Perhaps somewhere around when I recognize that I can feel her heartbeat echoing mine. I lose count of the beats, then I lose my grip on consciousness.

By the time I wake from the dream, I've lost feeling in one arm and both my legs, but I haven't lost *her*. So it's a trade-off I'm more than willing to make.

Chapter 22

I've actually been wearing it secretly since November 1st...

– Marcella

"Get over it," I say as I reach for another shiny red apple. My orange *engagement ring* winks in the sunlight, and Finn has been pretty much useless from the moment I put it on.

"Get over...what?" He drops the apple I hand him on the ground, not in the basket.

I scowl, and he snaps out of the daze long enough to look down.

Plucking the apple off the ground, he murmurs, "How did that get there?"

"A real mystery."

He's still fighting for a grasp on his brain cells when we cart our apples back to the barn to pay, so I say, "It's not a big deal. Stop staring, or I'll throw it in a lake."

"We're nowhere near a lake," he comments, quite magnanimously, as he hands over his card.

In the limo—while Finn holds my hand and examines the ring as though he didn't pick it out himself—I stare ahead at the bushels of apples on the seats across from us and mutter, "We bought enough apples to feed a small country. I think I got carried away picking them. Who knew twisting and snapping things was so fun?"

"A real wonder."

At home, with an apple skin noodle hanging out of my mouth, I toss baked slices into their crust beds and groan. "*Fine*. What do you want to say about it?"

Finn's smile turns on like a spotlight, blasting all the flesh off my bones. With perfect innocence, he says, "About what?"

Thankfully, Penny comes skipping into the kitchen before I follow through on the urge to throw the rest of my boiling apple compote on him. "Mm, pie!" she cheers. Without catching her breath, she presents me with a tiny canvas. "What do you think of this one?"

"Penny, I told you I don't have to approve every one you make."

She nods. "Right, right. Yes, of course. *But*, look!" She taps a fingernail to the tiny image. "*This* one has a little butterfly."

I stare at the itty bitty wings and have the inexplicable urge to keep it for myself.

"What's this?" Finn asks, drawing me from the trance.

"Wedding favors!" Penny tosses her head in his direction, and her short curls dance. "Marciboo hired me to make tiny easel paintings."

I clarify, "They're going to be set on actual tiny easels and decorate the reception place settings. They will then double as part of the favors people can take home."

"I *may* have quit my part time jobs in order to make several a day." Penny giggles. "I'm a *full-time* artist right now."

"Speaking of jobs, this is an elaborate scheme." I meet Finn's eyes. "And I need your help with it."

His brows rise. "Oh?"

"Since you don't have any friends but can invite whoever you want to your wedding with a decent chance they'll show, I'd appreciate it if you selected a handful of connections who will fall in love with Penny's work and make her a millionaire."

Finn blinks.

"It's very important to me."

He turns his attention to Penny. "Are you solely interested in traditional art?"

Her lips press together as her attention skids. "Well…" Her throat clears. "See…about that…"

I interject, "Penny likes to make a mess of anything and everything. She has been into traditional art, digital art, screen printing, jean painting, watercolor, charcoal—"

"I even know how to make logos! I've made about twenty-three logos for myself to reflect every time I shift my artistic focus into a new medium that I'm *positive* will be the *one*." She links her finger in a curl, which has a bit of butterfly wing paint on it. "It, um, never exactly is, though."

"Penny suffers from a chronic case of *I'll try that*, overburdened by a lack of immediate, raging success. Despite her ample skill, it is unfortunate that she never spends long enough on anything in order to build a dedicated audience for it."

Penny shrinks. "Ow."

"I've told you all this before. Consistency, trends, reliability. Finding your niche and sticking to it. If you want to make a career out of this, you need to embrace the *work* part."

"The boring stuff…"

"The *necessary* stuff. *Everything* is art, so the demand for artists isn't as underwhelming as the naysayers claim, but you need to focus your energy well enough to make more than a ripple in the pond of a thousand other unfocused minnows. Be the big fish who knows where she's going and keeps swimming."

Softly, Penny begins humming the *Finding Nemo* "Just Keep Swimming" song.

Finn switches his shaved apple out for a fresh one on the machine prongs and passes me a new skin snake. "Do you have a portfolio of some kind, Penny?"

Finishing the tune with an exaggerated facial expression, Penny beams. "I have a random stack of pictures I don't hate right now?"

"That sounds like an excellent portfolio." Finn grins.

When Penny trots off, I glare at my *fiance*.

Finn's back straightens. "What?"

"You're going to offer her a job yourself, aren't you?"

"It makes more sense than inviting random people to our wedding and hoping they think that's the appropriate time to peruse resumes, doesn't it? I have positions requiring artists, too. She puts a few years in at Marsh, then she has it on her resume alongside a glowing recommendation from me. Not only that, if I can, I'll put her in with a marketing team. Maybe she'll pick some things up there that she can use on a business of her own if that's the direction she wants to go."

Planting my elbows on the counter, I thread my fingers and lean toward Finn. "You scheming schemer, you. You make nepotism look ethical."

His eyes catch on my ring again. "Are you flirting with me?"

I blow at a spot of flour on his face, then reach to dust it off his forehead before conking him gently. "I would never do anything that cringe." Returning to my pie, I begin the tedious process of laying the lattices. "Thanksgiving is a week before the wedding and two weeks away. When I go wedding dress shopping later today, Mom will ask where we're spending it. I am prepared to tell her that all my aunts

185

and uncles and cousins who are flying in for Thanksgiving and staying through the wedding can see me *at* the wedding, because you want to know something *really* bad, *Finnegan*?"

His throat clears. "Not particularly?"

After placing the pie in the oven, I drag the pastry dough I've had rising since the start of this grand baking adventure to me, pull my ring off to set safely aside, and begin beating down the dough. "I still haven't met your mother, even though I *might* be marrying her son in a matter of days."

Finn's smile falters.

"Do you have any extended family I need to prepare to meet as well? I know when I asked you how many people you'd invite to the wedding, you said *maybe* ten, so I'm not expecting the same kerfuffle my family goes through on holidays, but ten people is ten people. And ten people I don't know are ten *strangers* I have to navigate. Also, now that I'm thinking about it, please tell me you got your *maybe ten* invites sent out? I don't think I followed up with you on that."

Focusing a bit too heavily on the apple he's rotating in the confines of the peeling machine, Finn murmurs, "I invited a few of my more enjoyable business relationships. Leopard, Pratt, Amare. With their plus ones. So my ten is actually six."

My mind sorts through the database I have compiled of Finn's business relationships. "You invited Levi, Velspar, and Leslie?"

He nods.

That should be interesting. I've only met Levi, the CEO behind Leopard, the largest growing social media site since MySpace collapsed into Facebook and Instagram, and the developer of my precious LeoPad. I'm half-sure that

Velspar is married to a singer-songwriter who's always topping all kinds of charts, but I've not met either of them. And Leslie? Well, Leslie is the leader of a body-positive fashion empire whose brand will be available at the boutique I'm going to this evening.

"I'll try to pick an Amare wedding dress later and I'll carry my LeoPad up the aisle in lieu of a bouquet. How am I going to explain the fact I don't know the lyrics to any of Velspar's wife's songs, though?"

"I think they'll understand if you show them your *Probs Need Therapy* playlist. They may even take it as a compliment."

Wow.

That was almost mean.

"Finn."

His gaze rises from where it settled on my ring. The emptiness in it sends a disturbance down my spine.

"What's wrong?" I ask.

His lips part, but before he can reply, Penny comes barreling into the kitchen, arms full of loose pages and random sketchbooks. Once she's done displaying her portfolio, I don't get another chance to address my unease before we have to rush to meet up with Mom and Brigid at the boutique.

Chapter 23

I should have planned to have you also wear a wedding dress, out of spite.

– Marcella

"It's *beautiful!*" Penny squeals when I step out onto the excessive catwalk with an excessive train and locate the excessive display of mirrors. I'd be inclined to believe Penny's assessment, save that her response has been the exact same every time I've pushed the curtain aside and exited in a new wedding gown.

Which, at this point in the evening, must be something I've done around five hundred times.

I am hot, sweaty, uncomfortable, and so over touching lace.

I can't believe I shaved for this.

Who even am I?

"Arms up," Brigid says.

I look at the itchy sleeves effectively gluing my arms down. If I try to fight the stiff fabric, it may tear, and then what will I do? Buy *two* several-thousand dollar dresses?

Absolutely I think not.

"Do not ask the impossible of me when I'm hungry," I mutter.

Brigid arches a brow. "You can't lift your arms?"

"Is lifting my arms actually mandatory?"

"If you don't want to be grouchy during the entire wedding, I think yes."

"Mm." Mom shakes her head and pushes back a lock of salted brown hair. "I agree with Bridge. If you can barely move, it's not going to be a fun time for you, and then you'll be irritable throughout the entire ceremony."

"These are wedding dresses." I reference the rows of white puffs surrounding us. "Nothing with long sleeves is going to be particularly durable."

"Sweetie," Mom says, lips pinching, "why are you so set on long sleeves? Think about *later*, after you have some kids and want to fit into your wedding gown again."

I narrow my eyes. "No. I don't want to. Getting married is one thing. Getting *pregnant*? That's something else entirely." I attempt to cross my arms, but guess who can't manage such a thing in this dress, either.

"It's true," my beautiful bud Brigid provides, with amicable coolness. "Children are sticky. You can't be trusted not to whack anything sticky that touches you into next week."

Penny giggles, clamping a hand to her mouth. "It wouldn't even need to be sticky. The last time Marciboo hit a child was embarrassingly recent."

"That's true." Mom pinches her chin. "Okay, I rescind the comment about kids. You should never be a mother, Marci."

Now I have to be one.

Out of spite.

Which probably means I really shouldn't be one, now that I'm thinking about it.

The thing is, Finn's form asked about children, and I did say I wanted a family...stickiness and all.

"I haven't hit a child for *at least* a year. And it's been

189

over a decade since it was *on purpose*." Huffing, I turn toward the mirrors and hate everything I'm looking at. "I'd be a good enough mother... Probably." Straightening myself as I catch my thoughts wandering, I snap, "*But that is not important right now.* The only thing I want to think about is that I planned an *outdoor* wedding at the end of *November,* and I don't want to be *cold.* It's long sleeves, or I'm wearing my butterfly wing cape. And that's *final.*"

Mom sighs. "That is *not* final. There are more options that you aren't considering. For instance..." She trails to a fluffy white bundle hanging in the corner beside the attendant who gave up on helping when I told her not to touch me. "...what about this?"

"Is that a dead animal?"

Void of emotion, the attendant chimes in, "It's faux fur."

"See? Fake. A fake fur shawl on something sleeveless will give you more mobility." Mom's lip juts. "I know it may be difficult for you to understand this, Marci, but I would like you to wear something comfortable enough to smile in."

My nose scrunches.

She displays a hand. "I know. I *know.* In a shocking turn of events, your mother wants wedding pictures where her daughter looks *happy.*"

Guess who can't put her hands on her hips, either?

It's me.

Arms straight down at my sides with disapproval, I lift my chin. "You expect far too much of me."

"Are you really going through with this?" Penny asks, having found her way to a section of blush pink dresses. "You actually want to marry Marshipan?"

Isn't that just the billion-dollar question?

Brigid snorts and tugs on my skirt. "Of course she does.

190

Do you really think anything less than *love* would get Marci into this much tulle?"

I look down at the abundant scratchy material and refuse to admit Brigid has a valid point.

My mom smiles. "I like Finn. He was very shy and polite when he talked with your father and me at the bonfire. I think we terrified him, which is an excellent sign given that he was the one with on-site bodyguards."

My eyes roll as I shuffle back into the dressing room to get out of this disaster. "Finn is a good person. A *really* good person. It's telling that the things I hate most about him are all stupid. Like, wow. I really need to grasp for reasons, don't I? He's just a genuine, kind person."

"Who is very, very hot," Brigid calls.

Penny adds, "And who has very nice hair!"

"Which adds to the hotness."

"It adds to his fluffiness," I mutter. "He has very fluffy, bright, bonkable hair."

Penny giggles. "It is as pretty as a wiggly duck butt."

My lips tug into a sardonic smile. "I agree." The second I've squeezed the dress down to my hips, my mom throws the curtain back.

Squeaking, I cover myself. "*Mom!* I'm *naked.*"

"Just like when I birthed you, idiot. Here." She shoves something silken, sleeveless, and splattered with autumn colors at me. "This is the one."

"Isn't this a bit—"

"Perfect?" Her trim brows rise. "Yes. It is. There's a cape that will cover your shoulders waiting for you out here. And there's a matching reception dress. So we can go straight to dinner after you're done making sure they fit."

Without letting me get another word in, my mother pulls the curtain closed, and I listen to her heels click her back to her seat at the end of the runway.

Getting dinner does sound better than sobbing over five hundred more dresses.

Never let it be said my mother and I aren't related. The genetics are loud.

After I change into the autumn gown, I *glide* from the dressing room and make my way down the cat walk, feeling exposed. "This is really expensive." I wrap my bare shoulders in a hug and scan for the previously mentioned cape.

"Boohoo." Mom twirls her finger. "What was the budget Finn gave you for this wedding again?"

I do my daughterly duty and spin, grumbling, "Half a million dollars...was mentioned...not really budgeted, exactly, though..."

"And how much have you spent so far?"

Less than a hundred thousand. Closer to fifty thousand. Because, honestly, who the heckish frick is spending *half a million dollars* on a *wedding*? I came distressingly close to having Taco Bell cater. Thankfully, my mother smacked me upside the head and told me to get Olive Garden instead. "I...do not want to tell you."

"Hm." She death stares at me. "Telling."

"You look like a *princess*!" Penny clasps her hands together and shines at me, eyes turning into literal stars.

"I agree," Mom declares, smiling brilliantly. "Is it comfortable?"

"It's about an inch too long."

"If only we hadn't started this endeavor by providing your measurements. Oh. Wait."

The sarcastic apple did not even roll when it fell from the tree.

I sigh, defeated. "It's comfortable, enough."

Mom crosses her arms and shakes her head at me. "I know, darling. It's so sad to be marrying into wealth."

My face heats as Brigid hands me the reception dress to try on. Gripping the padded hanger, I mumble, "I'm not marrying him for his money."

"And you *love* him, too? Well, that's just *depressing*." The woman pulls her purse into her lap and begins searching the pockets. "Let me see where I put my tiny violin. I thought I might need it again today, after I played it for your father, who was so sad he couldn't come to this fitting." She chuckles, evilly. "Sucks to be a boy."

I gape. "Wh—" I scowl. "You told Dad he couldn't come? He absolutely could have come. I wouldn't have cared."

Savage, Mom lifts her phone, presses a button, and overlaps the classical music whispering through the room with slow violin notes.

My arms fold, proving this dress's mobility far outranks that of the last monstrosity I was in. "You should be ashamed of yourself."

"And, yet, I'm not."

The apple.

It dropped dead on the roots.

Heaving a sigh, I march myself into the dressing room. "Mom. Invite Dad to dinner."

She turns the violin music up louder.

"If your father's coming, can I invite Cody?" Brigid asks.

"Yes." Sighing, I say, "Also, might as well tell Finn."

While I change, Penny sings "Alone Again (Naturally)" beneath the cacophony of classical and violin music, Brigid on the phone with Cody, and my heart trying to hammer its way out of my chest.

In two weeks…

I'm getting married to the man I love.

Chapter 24

I, Marcella Keyes, love you, Finnegan Marsh.

– Marcella

The first red flag I have ever seen Finn display appears on Thanksgiving morning. When he ignores my text asking what I should wear to dinner with his mother. Since he didn't tell me, it is a blow to my carefully-curated spite that I'm not in my pajamas when he rolls up with his *second* red flag.

Three words. Three *incriminating* words.

Before sitting *across from me* (a third red flag if I've ever seen one since we've started riding side-by-side like derpy little love birds), he said:

You look beautiful.

Finn, wisely, never makes unsolicited comments about my appearance. If he dares start talking about how I look without any prompting, I'll bite him hard enough to draw blood. For this reason, I know his little *comment* was a reply to my text.

Meaning he *saw* my text.

Meaning it was truly and completely ignored.

Bringing my red flag count up to a glorious *four*, he's been stiffly smiling out the window ever since. Not another word to me in the past thirty minutes.

I knew his mother lived a ways outside the city. I wasn't expecting to face the journey in dead silence, though.

Miraculously, however, I survive.

Just in time to experience red flag five through *I lost count...*

Nerves eat me up with every foreboding step I take toward what I can only call a *modest mansion*. Compared to Finn's and mine, the structure could pass as a normal house. If it weren't the only building at the end of a long, cobble drive past a gate, I could be convinced it belongs in a regular community, just perhaps the sort of *community* that winds up on a magazine cover.

The sticking dread that *something is wrong* pools in my gut as Finn knocks on the front door.

I've spent the past forty minutes gaslighting myself out of overreacting.

Finn's human. A person. With *feelings*, and so forth. He's allowed to be a little nervous about my meeting his mother days before we're scheduled to get married.

I do not need to make it my fault he's acting strange.

He has a life outside of me.

Besides, what's one ignored text? He probably saw it, was busy, forgot about it, and remembered the moment he came to pick me up. It's not like we talk constantly whenever we're together. This falls into the realm of normal behavior.

I'm just anxious because I'm *getting married* in a few days to someone I've only known for half a year.

I mean.

Come on.

I invited *my entire family*. I can't just say *sorry, no* in a back room now.

Ever since Finn made me feel safe and secure in the loudest, most chaotic, most *awful* place I have ever been, I've kind of…known. I had fun with him at the Halloween town. In the sort of place I wouldn't want to be within fifty miles of, I had *fun*.

Because I was with *him*.

Believing in something as idealistic as finding *the one* isn't like me. Logic dictates that many sorts of characters and personalities mesh with many other sorts. Finn isn't special and unique in a sense that no one else could ever make me feel safe and happy…but he is special, and he is uniquely him, and now that he has been the first person to put in the effort, he is *my* one.

Or something like that.

I don't know.

Barf.

How long have we been standing out here?

As though reading my mind, Finn clenches his fist and knocks on the door again.

This time, a woman with a tight smile greets us. "Mr. Marsh," she says, "I'm sorry. We were trying to get her settled in the dining room. Today's…not a good day."

"Is she all right?" Finn asks.

The woman opens the way for us to enter. "For right now. But…you may want to cut your visit short."

Finn's smile trembles, then—barely audible—he says, "Okay."

Sirens explode in my head as a chill soars down my spine. Without warning, Finn reaches his hand back, for me. His lips part, but I clasp on before he gets a chance to say anything.

His grip bites into my bones, but the pain is minimal compared to the shock my whole system is going through right now. With every step, the *stillness* buries into my flesh. With every step, the *wrong* mutates into something insurmountable.

He draws me through the pristine lobby to a small room with a round oak table. Seated there, with a bowl of ice cream, is an elderly woman I've seen before. Many times. In pictures. Tabloids. News stories.

The images I remember look nothing like this ghost of them.

It's as though she's been stripped of color.

Carefully, Finn approaches. "Hi, Mom."

Mrs. Marsh startles, and fear grips her glassy eyes. "Ulysses? Ulysses." Tears gather, bubbling over into her bowl. "You finally came home."

Ulysses...Marsh.

Finn's dad.

Finn's long since passed dad...

My heart shatters, turning to splinters in a pile near my toes.

Finn's voice breaks. "Mom, no. It's not Dad. It's Finn. Finny?"

Without registering his words, her eyes trail to me. "Who's this?" Her head begins to shake. "I told you we don't need any more help."

"She's not help." Finn pulls me to his side, grasps me around the waist, and forces the most painful smile I have ever seen. "Mom, this is my wife, Marcella."

Soundlessly, Mrs. Marsh repeats my name. "That's beautiful."

"It is. She is. I wanted you to meet her." His voice cracks. "I really...really wanted you to meet her." His other hand lifts, plunging into his hair. He grips the roots, and I feel the ways he's shaking in my entire body.

Setting my free hand against his shoulder, I pull on a

tried and true smile. "It's so nice to meet you, Mrs. Marsh."

"Wait." Confusion fills her gaze before a tear traces down her cheek. Broken, she whispers, "Wife? Did you say *wife*? But...*I'm* Uly's wife..."

It feels like I've swallowed acid. "Yes, you are. Do you remember Finn? Your son? I'm your son's wife."

Her brow furrows. "Finn's too young to have a wife. He's at his lessons right now. He's doing so, so well. I'm proud of him."

"What lessons are his favorite?" I ask.

"Math." The frailest start of a smile touches her lips. "He takes after his father. Loves his numbers. It's unusual for a boy his age to be so good with them. I wish he could make more friends... Will you be his friend, Mar...Mar... It was such a pretty name... So many letters. Finn likes letters. He says they have personalities..." Her tone drifts, tinny and...lost. "M was always his favorite."

The woman who greeted us at the door passes while I'm grappling for something to say. My memory on how to interact with someone suffering from Alzheimer's or dementia fails me more with every second. Turning to us, the woman says, "I'm sorry..."

I look at Finn, but he twists sharply on his heel before I can meet his damp eyes. Tripping after him as he makes his way back outside, I sort my emotions into clearly-marked boxes.

He didn't tell me.

He really should have told me.

What was he thinking?

His mother is...

His mother is dying.

He didn't tell me his mother was *dying*.

That's information I really needed to know and prepare for.

Finn stumbles on the last step off the porch, barely catching himself before we go careening into the concrete driveway. Once he's made sure I'm stable on my feet, he lets me go and starts pacing beside the limo, hands shaking. He taps his fingers against his thighs, deep breaths raking through his lungs.

"Finn—"

"I'm sorry." His voice chokes. "I didn't know how to tell you. I didn't know how to face it. I just...I hoped. I've been visiting her every week, watching her just...just *slip away*. She hasn't recognized *me* since October. Next, she'll...she'll forget how to eat...and...and then." He grips his face and closes his eyes. "They told me December, Marcella. *January.* February if we were really lucky. I—" He swallows. "We...aren't lucky."

A hollow pit opens up inside me. "You...you wanted to find a wife by the end of November so your mother could meet her?"

His blue eyes snap open, oceans pooling in them. Dropping his arm to his side, he says, "I wanted to find a wife...so I wouldn't be *alone* when my mother died." Words fracturing, he whispers, "As long as I can remember, I have been so...so...very lonely." He bites his lip—much too hard. "I can't buy friends, Marcella. I've tried. That isn't how it works."

"So you tried to buy love?"

A crackling laugh leaves him, ending abruptly as he wraps himself in a hug. "No. I tried to be honest about the social class expectations of applying to be my wife and included the deadline I saw creeping up on me, then I tried to find someone who would answer two hundred questions thoughtfully."

My fists clench at my sides. "For a billion dollars, what wouldn't people do?"

Finn smiles as tears coat his cheeks. "Save my parents." He shakes with every inhale. "I'm sorry, Marcella. You have every right to be upset. I'm sorry I didn't tell you. I just didn't know how to face making this real. And then I didn't know how to explain that the stress I've caused you with this time limit came down to a hope that my mother could make it to my wedding before she…" He can't force out the word *died*. "I didn't know how to tell you that I wanted a wife to fill the hole she has already left behind." Tossing his head back, he stares at the sky and whispers a swear. "It sounds…so terrible. Like all I've wanted is to use you. I'm sorry I never found the right words to explain myself, and now I've run out of time to try."

"Yeah." I close the short distance between us. "Expecting me to take her emotional place does sound awful."

"I'm sorry."

"Using me is also really cruel."

"I am so sorry."

I cross my arms. "So here's the part I can't figure out, Finn. Where in these past few months have I given you the idea that I want you to be *nice* to me?"

He stares. "What?"

"How many times have I asked you to be mean to me?"

His gaze wanders a moment as he runs his fingers through his hair. "A…concerning number."

"Exactly. You had this in your back pocket the *entire* time, and you *never once* thought to mention you were using me?"

His lips part. He blinks. His brow furrows. "Marcella, I'm confused. What are you trying to say?"

Stomping, I grab his hand, tight. "I'm *trying* to say you don't *ever* need to worry about me, Finn. Especially not right now, while you're hurting. I don't need pretty explanations. I will never expect your energy to pander to me, just like you better never expect any pandering in return. You have let me exist and given me more than I will ever need to cover anything I want. From the start, you told me you were doing this because you were lonely. Then? Then you made me fall in love with you. So *it's okay.* I don't mind being useful. Knowing I can do *something* for you when you've done everything for me isn't a bad thing." Tears burn in my eyes as I cup his damp face. "It's *okay,* Finn. I'm right here. And I'm going to stay right here. I don't think anyone can ever really *replace* anyone else, but I can promise that, for the rest of your life, you'll be subjected to my existence until you're completely sick of me."

"Never." He clamps his hand to my cheek. "I'll never grow sick of you. Not ever."

"Can I get that in writing?" I fight to form a small smile. "Because it's actually one of my biggest fears."

"Yes, you may." Dropping his forehead to mine, he whispers, "But only if I can get what you just said in writing, too. The part about how you're…how you're in love with me."

I let my lip jut. "No."

"Please?"

"Fine…" Wrapping my arms around him, I hold him as tight as I can. "I guess I can be convinced."

He crushes me in his embrace. "How romantic."

"In case you hadn't noticed, I'm not really the romantic one between us."

"Head kiss," he murmurs before crushing his lips to my hair. "Tell that to the flowers you pressed into that book on your dresser."

I scoff. "When did you go through my things?"

"While you were singing 'I Won't Say I'm in Love' in

201

the shower November 1st…" He nestles his chin against my head. "In my defense, it was left open."

"In mine, I have also kept every rock Bridge and Penny have ever given me."

Finn squeezes. "I'll give you a second to understand how that isn't a defense at all."

I huff. "Yeah, no. I heard it."

He swears, fighting down a swallow. "I'm so sorry about all of this… I don't know what I'd do without you. Thank you so much, Marcella. Just…just for being here with me, thank you."

Listening to his heart, I mutter, "Hey now…you'd be just fine. You'd probably buy a yacht and cry on it where no one could see you use hundred dollar bills to dab your tears. After pulling yourself together as much as possible, you'd descend into the kind of madness Disney Channel kids contract when they outgrow their shows. You'd be dyeing your hair even louder colors, getting face tattoos, and commissioning NASA to build you a luxury spaceship so you could circle the moon for funsies."

The weakest laugh in the history of laughs causes Finn's chest to tremble against my cheek. Seemingly unconvinced, he says, "Wow. You're right. You know me so well."

"It's true. But, unfortunately, I'm here." I grip his clothes as tight as I can. "So, I guess, instead of collapsing into an overfunded midlife crisis, we'll just have to get through this together instead. Is that…okay?"

He sniffles.

"I mean, if it's not, I'll dye my hair and circle the moon with you. Gonna have to pass on the face tattoos, though. I have a desk job. I'm sure you understand. My boss is a bit of a prick. Sometimes he even makes me do the job I signed up for."

Every muscle in him seems to sag, but I hear the incessant smile in his voice when he replies, "I'm sure your boss would understand if you tattooed his name on your face. Only because it might match yours on his."

I mumble, "I do hear our names have the same number of letters. And even the same number of syllables."

"Like someone planned it that way…"

"No one is that coordinated. We, Finnegan Marsh, are an adorable, drunk accident. And that's all there is to it."

He murmurs, "Marcella, does any of this imply that you're going to marry me next week?"

I hum. "You'll have to find out at the altar. On another note, my entire family has flown in for unrelated reasons. For similarly unrelated reasons, they're probably in my parents' backyard right now. With turkey." My nose scrunches. "That sounded insensitive, like I just want turkey, because I expected turkey when we came here, and I will be honest. I *do* want turkey…but what I'm really trying to say is that while the turkey will probably be cold and dry by now, my family will be just drunk enough to be funny. And, still unrelated to your previous inquiry, they're probably about to become your family, too. So it's very important to begin gathering blackmail on them. If that would make you feel better. I can organize to take notes in the car."

He exhales a damp laugh into my hair. "That's…a very tempting offer. But I kind of don't want to be around people right now."

"Such a mood. I respect that."

"You're not people. Just in case you thought I'd be dropping you off at home or with your family."

I let all my weight rest into him. "You know something? That wasn't even a concern that crossed my mind."

"Marcella?"

"Yes, love?"

He squeezes me, and even though his voice is still thick with emotion, his weak smile hasn't faltered since it returned. "Can we pick up something to eat on the way home, grab my laptop, and play Stardew together in your room?"

Breaking away when he begins to, I grin up at him. "Dibs on the couch."

Chapter 25

I, Finnegan Marsh, will never, ever, grow sick of you,
Marcella *Marsh*.

— Finnegan

"Dude," Cody says as he adjusts my tie and jacket. They're both crooked. Which is fairly unlike me. But I'm *getting married in twenty minutes*, so perhaps an exception to the rule is allowed. Unless, of course, I'm *not* getting married in twenty minutes. Marcella could still change her mind at the altar. Cody pushes his glasses up his nose. "Calm down."

"What if she reaches me, and her father steps away, and she takes a good, long look, then says, *actually, nah?*"

Cody echos, "Actually, *nah?* Are you serious?"

I have never been more serious in my life. "I think I'm panicking. She would absolutely prank me on my wedding day. Probably to get back at me for taking all the olives out of her grandmother's homemade sauce yesterday at family dinner. It's just...*who* puts *olives* in their pasta sauce?"

"Sometimes that woman also adds peas."

My mouth drops open as I look at my best man. "I'm sorry. *Why?*"

He shrugs. "Who knows? The real question is why did a container end up at my house... Anyway, I think you're

205

going into withdrawals." He tightens my tie and brushes off my dress shirt before straightening the orange flower in my pocket. "Brigid tells me you and Marci haven't left each other's side since Thanksgiving."

"That's not true." When Marcella asked if I needed to shower with her, my brain shut off. By the time I escaped the coma, she had a towel turban and was kissing my nose. "We've respected each other's privacy."

"Privacy." Cody frees a heavy sigh. "I remember privacy. Privacy disappears once you're married. Brigid has entire conversations with me while I'm on the toilet. I don't understand why she thinks that's the appropriate time to chat, but with my odd hours, I guess I'm just glad she wants to spend whatever time she can with me."

I don't foresee Marcella and I ever sharing a bathroom, but I also didn't foresee her being such a cuddler. This morning, she was so latched on, her feet didn't touch the ground until I was finished brushing my teeth. Shortly after, she remembered we were getting married today, so she kissed my cheek, unwound, and was gone.

I haven't seen her since she swiped a serving-size spoonful of ice cream for breakfast.

Hm. Okay, fine. Maybe this is withdrawals.

Or maybe it's easier to blame my nerves on something I don't actually feel the need to worry about. I've never been anxious where it concerns Marcella. I've never been afraid. From the start, she's been a well of overflowing safety. Focusing on my raging codependency means I don't have to think about how vacant my side of the aisle will be, how my father and mother...won't be here.

My attention lifts to the mirror, finding myself, Cody, Mark, and Jeff. My always stoic bodyguards nudge one another and chat at the back of the room. Even with their low voices, it's quiet in here. And I'm not smiling.

The ache inside my chest isn't what I expected to feel right now. I hoped I'd be overcome with joy. I'm marrying *Marcella*. The woman I love. I get to spend my life with her, but there's still so much pain I can't shake. I don't know how many days my mother has left. I don't know if she'll be gone by the time we return from our honeymoon. I don't know if I'm a terrible son for not knowing how to face these final moments.

She's not recognized me since October.

She's stuck with a picture of me that I haven't been for years.

Knowing that Marcella won't let me be alone doesn't mean I won't miss my mother so much more than words can explain. It helps, knowing I have her, but it still hurts.

A knock sounds on the door, and Brigid calls in, "It's time for you, Marshi. Get outside, stat."

My chest hurts.

Cody says, "Are you ready?"

To marry my best friend? "Yeah, I think so."

Together, we leave the groom preparation room and find our way to the decorated venue. Marcella didn't opt for what I'd consider a *luxury* wedding in the sense that the charges I saw come through added up to less than a hundred grand, but…

Wow.

She picked a grove at the height of autumn. Brilliant leaves scatter the grass, landing on her friends and family, landing on my empty chairs. The sparse, bright trees aren't thick enough to block out the sun, which winks off the silk butterflies adorning everything. I stop myself beneath the arbour, in front of the officiator, and do my best to keep my heart inside my chest as I look down the lane of bright cloth marking the space between the two clusters of chairs.

Frozen in place, I wait.

Once the processional music begins, I find it in myself to smile.

The first glimpse of Marcella in her wedding gown steals all the air from my lungs.

On my side of the aisle, Leslie elbows her husband in the gut and beams, letting me know that, perhaps, I have her to blame for designing the dress Marcella is wearing. The extravagance certainly lends itself to the Amare brand.

I have never seen anything so beautiful before in my life.

As everyone stands and the music shifts into what I swear is one of Marcella's therapy songs adapted into a wedding march, I find myself fixated.

Barefoot, Marcella floats up the aisle, over the soft orange petals I barely registered one of her younger cousins throwing moments ago. Her gown—white, spun with autumn vines, and dusted around the hem with the vague idea of spices—billows in a breeze that teases the cape around her shoulders.

My hands are shaking when her father passes her to me.

To *me*.

Forever.

Once she's given her waterfall bouquet of flaming orange to her mother, who is acting as both maid of honor and mother of the bride, she *smiles*.

It's a wicked sort of smile. The kind that indicates she knows my organs are struggling to keep me alive right now. But it's still so beautiful I can hardly comprehend it.

The classic vows the officiator feeds me exit my dry mouth, stale, and it takes every ounce of my willpower to keep from going off script and waxing poetic on all the ways I believe this woman—who is standing in front of me right now with her arms folded—has saved my life.

My brain short circuits when I hear: "Marcella Keyes,

you've prepared your own vows?"

Her lashes flutter as my attention whips to our officiator, to her, to the audience, then back to her. I mouth *what*, but she is a cold, heartless little imp with the smuggest smile in the world, and I am wholeheartedly, disastrously in love with her.

"Finnegan Marsh," she begins, uncrossing her arms to cross them the other way, "it's been six months since I met you, in an office that had fish swimming in the floor. Interviewing with you while you clicked your pens and twisted in that—" She swears. "—chair of yours was actually quite almost my thirteenth reason. Working for you those first two months resulted in many pints of ice cream consumed. Most of them donated by my friends, because I lived in generational poverty, begging a merciful God to maintain my AC better than I maintained my health. I sincerely do not know why you thought I was qualified for the position of being your assistant. I can only imagine my presentation on how I color-code schedules surpassed your expectations. Let me confess now: that habit of planning ahead is caused by unmedicated anxiety." She loosens a hand from her crossed arms just enough to touch her chest with all the grace of a princess. "Today, you are marrying a disorder, but I hope you already know that, otherwise I'm going to be very embarrassed."

When she pauses, I stammer, "I don't think—"

"Yes, you do. Don't be so hard on yourself."

Laughter bubbles up in my chest, so I bite my lip and fight the smile overwhelming me. It is nearly as forceful as the threat of tears.

"Finn," she continues, "thank you for loving me. Even though I'm guarded. Even though I find it hard to accept perfectly adequate people for the dumbest things. *Thank you* for telling me it is okay to protect myself until I feel

209

safe enough to let my walls down and admit that it's really not all that annoying when you twist in your chair or when you separate all your food by primary colors or when you..." She blinks, and her attention drifts skyward. "No actually, I'm adamant about the pen clicking. That one you will need to stop or do out of hearing range, lest I murder you in your sleep. I've gone off topic. What I'm saying is, I've grown accustomed to the *hate them before they hate me* mentality. But when you saw me, *for* me, you didn't hate it." She lowers her face, blows out a breath, and contains herself. "I don't know how I'll ever understand that, but I can promise to love you forever for it." Squaring her shoulders, she clears her throat. "Today, we're both missing people who should have been here—your parents...my brother—and I know I can't fix that."

My heart clenches, and she unravels her arms to clasp my hand.

"I know I can't fix a lot of things." She squeezes my fingers. "I'm not rich. I don't have a glowing personality. I'm anal about too much stupid stuff. I really don't have anything to offer you in a relationship. But...there is something I have that I'm willing to share, if you're okay with it. It's pretty second-hand, and it comes with olives in the tomato sauce, but it's..." She frees a wet laugh. "... well, it's actually quite unequivocally the best." Turning to her side of the aisle, she says, "My cousins."

In an uncoordinated stream, a dozen people stand, wrangle children, and cross the aisle to my side.

"My aunts. My uncles. My grandmother."

The procession repeats, more people moving across the petal-strewn lane to my side. A teardrop hits the flower in my pocket.

"My parents' friends, who said they wanted to come to a fancy wedding when my mother blabbed about it."

210

A handful of people laugh as they stand and join my seats.

Marcella looks behind her, at Penny and Brigid. "My best friends."

They cross to stand behind me, tapping my shoulder as though I'm not already struggling with everything in me not to sob.

"My mom."

A swear hisses past my lips as I look at the sky. It's perfect. Blue. Beautiful and full of soft white clouds.

The woman shows no mercy as she sweeps in to hug me tight before standing firmly behind me, a hand on my back.

"And, my dad."

He stands on my other side, clasping his hand over his wife's. I feel them both through my suit jacket—an overwhelming presence.

"Finnegan Marsh," Marcella says, tears in her eyes, "I hope you know that once you marry me, you won't ever have the luxury of being alone again. You're entirely too lovable. And I give it half a reception before all the poor saps you didn't meet at dinner last night are under your spell." She sniffs, huffing. "I say *half* because you and I will be leaving early. I am *already* tired."

Laughter encases me as I fall utterly apart.

Forgetting myself and the order of things, I kiss Marcella a bit too early. Before my hand can find her hair, I swear into her mouth and pull back. "Sorry," I exhale. "Sorry."

Chuckling, our officiator says, "Mr. Marsh, you have something you wanted to present?"

This time, Marcella gets to look surprised.

"Yes, I do." I battle for stability amid the rushing tides of everything Marcella is and everything she has brought

211

into my life. Reaching in my pocket, I withdraw a box decorated in ocean blues. "With any luck at all," I begin, "we've reached our ten heart event, so according to the laws of *Stardew Valley*, you have to accept this."

As Marcella's mouth falls open, I reveal the corkscrew shell necklace dubbed the *Mermaid's Pendant* in the game and defined as *the item used to propose marriage to a marriage candidate*.

"What do you say?" I ask.

"*Stop*," she whispers, clasping her hands to her mouth. "This is like *the* dream."

"Is that a *yes*?"

She leaps into my arms. "It's an *I do*."

And, then, our officiator says, "You may kiss the bride."

But, this time, she kisses me.

Epilogue

Sincerely, Yours.

– Marcella

Finn's eyes sparkle like two fancy smancy champagne flutes over his armful of two incredibly fat stuffed chickens with square eyes. The longer I stare at him, daring him to explain why he's interrupting me during work when his schedule says he's supposed to be answering the emails I forwarded to him an hour ago, the wider his grin.

"What's with the chickens?" I ask.

"They're Stardew chickens. Your favorites. The blue and black ones."

I hum. "I did absolutely notice that. Which is problematic. Because that probably means they're for me, and you are on a *buying me things* ban ever since I made a joke about hating how our bedroom is on the top floor and I'm too tired in the morning to survive walking downstairs, and—"

"And I put in a slide. I *know*." His eyes roll.

I smile.

He got that little trait from *me*.

And, as I bite my lip, I'll give you one guess as to what I've picked up from him…

He continues, "That was three weeks after we got back

from our honeymoon on the island, and I've behaved myself ever since, haven't I?"

"I would say *yes*, but the proof that you haven't rests before me. Like an adorable bruise."

Heaving a sigh, Finn sets the chickens down atop my keyboard, leans over my desk, and grips my chin in his palm. He stretches my neck while I forget absolutely everything I'm upset about. "Pumpkin," he murmurs, "do you know what today is?"

"November 30…ohhh…" I press my lips together. "It's our anniversary, isn't it?"

"Indeed it is, my love."

"Well then. That is unfortunate. For you." I begin to stand. "Mr. Marsh, I'd like to take some time off for a special occasion."

"Sit down."

I pop my sweet little rump back in my seat and pout.

"Don't give me those eyes," he murmurs.

"Why not? They're big and brown for a reason."

He sighs and has the audacity to move himself behind my desk with me, where he rests against the edge and curls a few fingers in my hair before tugging on the strands. "The reason cannot be to torment me."

"Can," I say. "Is."

Leaning forward, he kisses the locks of my hair, then my cheek, then my forehead—whispering each location before his lips land. His thumb swipes my bottom lip when he moves back, and for a breathless moment I think he's about to be mean to me. We have been working on it, after all. Once, last week, he went out to get food and pretended he didn't get me any when he got back.

I had the *best* time stealing his dinner while he smiled and let me. Even though he should have wrestled me to the ground over that handful of french fries…

214

But, anyway, as I said: we're still working on it.

"You didn't forget," he says at long last. "You don't forget things."

"I don't forget grudges. Or vendettas. My spite is immortal. But fluffy little anniversary dates? Why do I need to remember those when we're together all day, every day?" I smile pretty and tilt my head away from his grip so my hair pulls. "What could we even do that would be special?"

"Break the buying you things ban." He threads his fingers at the base of my head, twists, and tugs, lifting my face so he can plunge in for a kiss. "Take you out to dinner with our new chicken children."

"*Our?*" I whisper against his lips. "We have to *share* them?"

"Duh."

My stomach flutters. "That was an *excellent* duh. Almost demeaning. Which has *mean* in it. I'm so proud."

He squishes our noses together, whispering seductively, "I've got it. I know what we can do that would be phenomenally special."

"Finnegan Marsh, if you say *go to therapy*, we are getting a divorce, and you didn't have me sign a prenup, so I hope you don't mind that I'm taking the island."

"First you steal my heart, now you steal my jokes. What's next? My liver?"

"Hearts sell for the most on the black market, and you know you handed me yours on a platinum platter. Theft was not involved."

He kneels, places his hands on my knees, and looks up into my eyes. "I did do that, didn't I?"

"Well, okay. *Hand* is a stretch. You kind of chucked it at me, like a frisbee, and I didn't know what to do with myself for several business days."

215

His fingers tap, tap against my thighs. "It's very cute that you know what sells well on the black market."

I comb my nails through his pretty hair. "How else do you think I wooed you, if not with my random, disturbing knowledge of concerning topics?"

The elevator to the top floor dings, and I look up to find my beautiful friends stepping out with their husband and, ever since the wedding last year, bodyguard boyfriend. Mark escorts Penny up to the desk like a princess in paint-stained overalls, and she tosses her sunglasses up into her curls like the model she's always been. "Did we arrive too soon?" She flicks her finger between my husband and I. "You two look like you're still flirting."

Finn peeks over the top of my desk, past a blue chicken butt. Rising, he says, "We're just about to wrap it up. Too soon for what, though?"

"The triple date Marciboo planned."

Brigid interjects. "We're getting food then learning knife throwing."

Finn tilts his head back toward me and my folded arms...while I twist my stupid chair back and forth, back and forth. "Forgot, huh?" he accuses.

"No comment on the knife throwing?"

"I shall take great care that I don't grow into a complacent husband."

Penny's musical laughter fills the office floor, and she turns her smile on Finn. "Did you tell her yet?"

"Tell me what yet?" I say as I pull a chicken into my lap and squish it.

Finn says, "Nope. That's a surprise for after."

My eyes narrow. "I hate surprises. What have you done?"

He extends his hand. "It's mean not to tell you, isn't it?"

216

Ignoring his hand, I rise and remind him, "You're very bad at being mean."

"Because I don't practice enough."

Brigid checks her phone. "Guys, I thought you were wrapping this up. We're going to be late if we don't get going. We have a reservation."

Finn plants a firm hand at my waist and guides me around my desk. "Marcella hates being late."

"Marcella hates a grand number of things," I say, snatching my other chicken so neither will be lonely during the ride to dinner. "That is perhaps my single defining trait."

Finn glances down at me for many long moments, chuckles, and says, "Nah. Not even in the top ten."

How dare he.

Nevertheless, I'm smiling all the way to the limo, where he breaks and tells me he bought me something else for us to parent. Something I've wanted for a long, long time. Something that makes Cody's face twist in abject disgust.

Shrieking with uncharacteristic glee after my husband shows me the most perfect, most precious, most darling picture of a baby corn snake *ever*, I dive into his arms—and bite him while I kick my legs.

Extended Epilogue

Always and forever.

– Finnegan

Marcella's foot rests on my shoulder while I rub the other in my lap. Sprawled on the couch in the main living room, which is overburdened with Christmas decorations, she groans and plays with her little corn snake, which I gave her less than thirty days ago.

She already loves it more than me.

"Finnnn?"

"Yes, love?"

Awkwardly flopped, she struggles to lift her head and scowl. "Do you think maybe you could just…I don't know." Her eyes narrow. "*Snap* my ankle?"

I drop my attention to her perfect little foot. "No, I don't think that's something I'm wholly capable of."

She pokes me in the ear with her toe. "Why not? You weak or something?"

"Compelled, by love, not to hurt you."

Her sigh pours into the low Christmas music playlist I started an hour ago, despite her protest. "That is very disappointing behavior."

"You'll get over it." I move my attention up her calf, kneading into the muscle. "Probably."

"Unlikely. Do you even know me?"

I do. Quite intimately. And that knowledge may forever fill my soul with peace.

"It's Christmas dinner. With your wonderful family. In the beautiful house we bought your parents last Christmas. Why don't you want to go?"

"Can I say *olives in the marinara*?"

"That's a me problem. You *like* the olives in the marinara."

Seemingly upset by this truth, she pets Copper the corn snake's tiny head. "I don't want to go because my stupid parents invited my stupid extended family to their stupid new house for this stupid holiday, so they will be bringing stupid gifts."

"Yes, and so are we…"

"Right. But we have *cool* gifts because I pay attention to my silly little relatives. They're going to give me sweaters and candles and garbage that I'll have to pretend to like while everyone stares at me. Worse, I'm rich now, so not being blissfully overjoyed will make everyone hate me and think I'm a snob."

"Your family does not strike me as the type to hate you, especially not when you went through the trouble of stalking their social media pages and identifying the best gifts for each person. The attention to detail made me fall in love with you all over again."

"If you really loved me, you'd snap my ankle so I don't have to go. Send my most pathetic regards. Bring the pastries we made yesterday as an apology."

I frown. "No. Those are mine."

"I can stay here and make you more."

"With a broken ankle? What kind of husband would I be to abandon you in such distress then demand you make me pastries amidst your pain?"

Her smile brightens her dark eyes until they're glittering. "A very, very *mean* one. My biggest dream. The best Christmas gift."

I tut. "What a shame you forbade me from getting you Christmas gifts."

"This is an exception. Besides, would it *really* be a Christmas gift if I've been asking for it for so long?"

"If it's given at Christmas, yes."

She rolls over, twisting her leg in my hands, and mutters incoherently about *social constructs*. When she's finished, she lifts her head and declares, "*Pickles*. Get thee hence without me. Apologize on the behalf of your temperamental wife. Say I was livid and started threatening to throw knives at you."

"They wouldn't believe me."

Casting a look over her shoulder, she arches a brow. "Why not? It's a very believable thing for me to do."

"Too believable to end with threats. I'd require a stab wound."

Unpretzeling herself, very careful not to hurt Copper, Marcella scoots closer to me on the couch. "Finn…"

"No."

Her lip juts. "You don't love me anymore?"

I pinch her chin. "You may stab me *tomorrow* if it so pleases you. But never to get out of meeting with your family, who loves you, very much. Also, using the safe word flippantly is not allowed in this household. I'm putting my foot down, on behalf of our son."

She melts herself into my side, head plopping atop my shoulder. Letting our son curl around her wrist, she mutters, "I don't know if you deserve it right now, but I got you a gift."

"I got you one, too."

"You suck."

I murmur, "Forehead," then kiss her there. "I love you."

Huffing, she stands and marches away. When she returns, she has exchanged Copper for a scrapbook. Unceremoniously, she drops it on my lap, folds her arms, and peers down her nose at me. "I didn't wrap it, because that's dumb."

My lips part as I turn to the first page.

Our First Year Together

Pictures. Notes. Memos.

My throat closes as I take every tediously-placed item in.

Our wedding.

Our honeymoon.

My...mother. A tribute to her, using the photos from the funeral.

"You made this?" I whisper.

Her eyes roll as she bites her lip. "No. I hired someone. Of *course* I made it." She stabs her finger to a lipstick mark beside pictures from our New Year's party. "I kissed the page myself. Right here. With all the love in my wee black, shriveled heart."

One of these days I'm going to sit my precious wife down and show her all the things she does to care about people and get her to stop talking like this. One of these days, she'll get a college research paper on the subject, and I'll quiz her on every bullet point. Starting with *exactly how many rocks do you have in a bucket by our bed?* And *why do you obsessively count them so often?*

Mm. Yeah. That's what I thought.

Wee black, shriveled heart, my foot.

"Do you like it?" she asks.

"Completely." Gently, I keep turning the pages, awestruck. Finally, the last one contains the memos we sent each other the day after our anniversary.

Sincerely, Yours.

Always and forever.

"We're going to be late," Marcella mutters while I'm busy tracing the script all over the page around the printed notes. She's written little unhinged comments like: *You're never getting rid of me* and *Stuck together, eternallyyy.* In one corner, she's simply doodled an evil face surrounded by chaotic laughter, and I didn't know it was possible to love her more.

But here I am.

Falling harder each day.

"Finn. We're going to be late," she repeats.

Pulling my gaze from the most beautiful gift I've ever received, I say, "What about your gift?"

"Won't I be tortured enough at my parents' house?"

"Nope." Moving my scrapbook aside, I pat my lap.

Deeply disgruntled, she plops down.

I wrap her up in my arms and press a hard kiss to her jaw, squeezing her until she relaxes. "What I got you pales in comparison to this."

"Good. I prefer to be underwhelmed."

"I commissioned Penny."

She twists, looking at me. "Penny still works for you. Is it really a commission if you ask her to do something on salary?"

"I paid her extra. And nitpicked the piece to death. She hated me by the end of it."

Marcella's arms fold. "Hating you is my job. No one else is allowed."

I nestle in. "Unfortunately, you've left a vacancy for many months now."

"Can't be right. Sometimes, you click your pens in earshot, and I allot a special time to hate you for it on the weekends. Where's my picture?"

"Under the couch. I didn't wrap it either."

She moves to look, finds the canvas, and gasps as she pulls the large portrait out into the Christmas lights. "Butterfly fairy princess," she whispers.

"With her butterfly fairy prince," I note.

A wide smile overtakes her. "You know, butterflies don't mate for life. Even though their lives are so short. Isn't that sad?" She traces my likeness on the portrait with a delicate fingertip. "I'm glad we're not butterflies. I want to spend so much longer with you."

"To think when we first started dating you were counting down the days." I stare at the *back* of the canvas, where a suspicious comic of Marcella stabbing me with a dirty knife rests. "I'm so glad you changed your mind."

Her eyes meet mine. "I've told you before. People don't change; they grow. You gave me the space I needed to thrive. You taught me I wasn't hard to love. Loving you after that was easy. I kind of just…grew into it."

Warmth spreads throughout my entire body. "And I'm so glad you did…but…pumpkin."

She wiggles, looking at her picture. "Yeah?"

I grin, knowing we are going to be *so* late. "Turn that around, love."

Read the rest of the Cinnamon Rolls and Pumpkin Spice Series!
Each book is a standalone, full-length, closed-door romance that can be read in any order.

Hating the Cinnamon Roll CEO by Camilla Evergreen
Falling for Autumn (Again) by Jen Atkinson
Paris, Pumpkins & Puns by Marion De Ré
Fall With Me by Amanda P Jones
Cinnamon & Spice Conundrum by Leah Busboom
Cinnamon Roll Set Up by Genny Carrick
Coffee Break with the Billionaire by Holly Kerr
The Friendly Fall by Kristine W Joy

Made in United States
Troutdale, OR
10/30/2024

24307737R10142